Lean Six Sigma

The Ultimate Beginner's Guide to Learn Six Sigma. Boost your Business or Startup with the Lean Six Sigma Method.

Anthony O'Brien

Introduction

A higher rate of customer satisfaction is desired by every business. Reaching that goal is much difficult than it sounds, this book contains the guide you need to reach your goal by using Lean Six Sigma methodologies. The goal that you seek is attainable by implementing what this book has to offer for your business.

Lean Six Sigma is a step by step guide for you to boost your business to its maximum potential. The methods you will learn here will give your business higher productivity, enhanced functionality, and improved process timing with less wastage of material.

On implementation of Six Sigma to your everyday business routine, you will notice an improvement in the overall functionality of the business processes. You will find the same range of output every single time with no variance in production efficiency.

Six Sigma combined with the Japanese Lean Production method becomes a highly efficient production process known as Lean Six Sigma. This book will elaborate on every aspect of Lean Six Sigma to help you learn better.

Six Sigma divides into two methodologies DMAIC and DMADV with both dealing in different aspects of production processes while having their own implementation phases. Lean production and Six Sigma or Lean Six Sigma, when put together in any industry's working process, can maximize a company's potential.

Lean production focuses on reducing wastage while making sure the quality is maintained at all times.

Lean Six Sigma focuses on eliminating defects from a production process while also reducing wastage. Following Lean Six Sigma methodology will give you a faster, better, and efficient production process with little to no wastage of your resources.

The book is divided into six parts covering the various needs of your business. The starting chapters of this book will make you aware of the history and the present of the Six Sigma and give a better understanding of the method. Once all that has been covered the book makes you aware of your ultimate goals and how to reach it in the most efficient way.

Next, you get to know how you can benefit the maximum from the process and how its principle can fill the gaps in your business. Then comes the part where you understand the different methodologies of Six Sigma and their different approaches to help your business reach its full potential.

Further along the way, you get to learn from the mistakes of others on using Lean Six Sigma and how you can avoid them while understanding which parts of your business need improvement. The book ends with the critics about Six Sigma while making it easy for you to know how to get yourself Six Sigma certified.

By reading this book, your thinking about your company's structure will change drastically. You will have a different point of view about your company's strategic level as well as your front line supervisors. You will never see a fault as a crack in your system but a tool to improve the overall balance of your company.

The change in your view will lead to a better result while impacting the working of your employees in a positive way.

As the business world is becoming more and more about the survival of the fittest, it is a wise move to do business as a team rather than going alone in the competition.

The competition is getting tough day by day as new entrepreneurs are always in search to skyrocket their business. Such actions from newcomers demand continuous improvement from every business that wishes to compete in the long run.

Lean Six Sigma brings out the very meaning of an efficient business which is to yield maximum profit with minimum resources.

You can achieve a lot more by making yourself aware of the benefits of Lean Six Sigma. Before we go into it, understand that no change can take place overnight and every great journey starts with a single step.

This book is key to open new doors for your business by giving you the knowledge of efficient methodologies that can be implemented in your business.

Chapter I: The Origin of Six Sigma

The Story of Six Sigma

Evolution has always been parallel to humans since the day mankind has stepped on earth. The human race has been evolving as long as we know our history. For humans, the most noticeable development since history has been agriculture and still is up to this very day. But what happened in the mid of the 18th century has defined our very future.

The first industrial revolution began in the middle of the 18th century to the early 19th century, in a few European regions. The very first industrialization was observed in Great Britain followed by Switzerland, Germany, and France respectively. The shift from an agrarian culture to industrial culture brought a lot of change in people's thinking.

The change in thinking

The industrial revolution brought new sets of machines. The machines worked faster and better replacing the average working human. On one hand, the new age of machines was making its way to the market. On the other hand, it was unconsciously transforming humans' demands. It was giving birth to the concept of efficient production.

People started thinking more competitively as they shifted from physical labor to mental labor. Having more time to think about improving the process for efficient production, researchers started working on improving the production process as much as possible.

The focus shift

The focus shifted from efficient production to efficient production process with higher quality products. The basic purpose industry was clearly in people's minds to transform inputs into outputs. Researchers were now focused on producing higher quality products with higher efficient production techniques.

Since the beginning of industrialization, industries have been making improvements to their methodologies through the introduction of new standards to new procedures for production. Industries have been doing it all to reach maximum efficiency in their production line.

Numerous standards have been brought up by various researchers to make a perfect standard for the production process. The one, however, which is globally recognized and acknowledged, is Six Sigma.

What is Six Sigma?

Six Sigma is a procedure that assists organizations to concentrate on developing near-perfect services and products.

Six Sigma is an expression derived from Statistics. Sigma is a statistical quantity of variation for output.

Six times Sigma (or Six Sigma) means the 99.999% accuracy of production within a million opportunities. The expression accuracy percentage means to have 3.4 defects per million products or services. A Three Sigma level quality states to have 93.32% accuracy within a million opportunities. In simple words, it allows having 67,000 defects per million.

Six Sigma follows a progressive reduction of defects through:

- Identifying root causes of error occurring
- Making sure the crucial root cause is identified
- Making use of corrective action

The minimization of defects will eventually lead to better profitability and customer satisfaction. The process can be summarized as a reduction in defects leads to improvement in yield to satisfied customers and improvement in overall profitability.

TQM and ISO

A crucial aspect of Six Sigma is that it can get along well with other initiatives like ISO 9000 and TQM. The difference in Six Sigma is that is more focused on customers than the operations of the company. It focuses on outcomes that ultimately lead to the satisfaction of customers.

ISO 9000 defines the guidelines on quality management systems that focus on improving performance but they aren't meant to give certification.

TQM focuses on a few key elements which together form the word "PRECEPT".

- Prevention
- Right first time
- Eliminate waste
- Continuous improvement
- Everyone's concern
- Participation
- Teamwork and empowerment

Brief History and Present of Six Sigma

Six Sigma's birth can be traced back to the 18th century, the reason was mass production with quality. The statistics upon which the theory is based have been around for a longer period of time.

The core principle of statistical theory as used in the Six Sigma was developed by a German mathematician Friedrich Gauss. He described it in his Normal Distribution curve or Bell Curve. The answers lie on the normal distribution of one standard deviation multiples, far from the mean, represented with the Greek alphabet Sigma 'σ'.

The framework of statistical quality control, products and procedures are measured and calculated to know the variation form the known standards while the spread of distribution indicates the difference.

Six Sigma was first developed by Motorola in the USA in 1985 to help develop a defect-free pager.

The Industrial Revolution and rise of Six Sigma

Before the industrial revolution quality management and quality, the inspection was a costly matter. Quality workmanship was acknowledged, the only way to get a quality product was to pay a higher price for it. On the other hand, supervision wasn't required making the process less tiring.

The world changed with the Industrial Revolution. The goods were being produced at a faster rate now and it was the time when Eli White a well-known American inventor of cotton gin got an idea from "interchangeable parts, first expressed, by Honor le Blanc".

When given a contract of making 10,000 muskets for the French government, Eli developed standardized musket parts so that the other products do not vary off from the standard and can be produced for years to come. This steered the industry towards the age of mass production.

Whitney's implementations defined the Uniformity System which was put to use by the defense establishments and military-industrial complex across the Americas and Europe. Such development is noticeable in the history of industrial production as it was a step towards mass production while taking care of the quality.

The Story of Motorola

The idea was to hitch product design to process quality and ensure a product only went into design when the specifications were up to the standards expected by process control.

In order to stay with the time and to boost the confidence of companies. The Malcolm Baldridge National Quality Award was introduced in the United States, and Motorola Corporation won the first time out of all, in 1988.

At the starting of the 1980s, Motorola began quality practices when the firm was trying to renovate its pocket pager business. The company was under the leadership of Bill Smith and Bob Galvin, Motorola chartered a policy of using statistical quality control to devices and not only process capability but also to the product details. Bob Galvin and Bill Smith are considered to be the managers who first proposed the idea of continuous quality improvement.

To assist the new model, Motorola expanded the older notion of three sigma by three additive sigma from the mean to also comprise product specifications and hence giving birth to the term Six Sigma.

The spread of Six Sigma statistically speaking means to have 99.99% of all output resulting in 0.02 defects per million opportunities making it efficiently zero.

Motorola also started to make use of statistical methods of control. Data tools like CpK and Cp (process capability index) and (process potential index) respectively were used in for the first time in quality management to define the policy at the maximum levels. Using the precise quality targets like 3.4 defects per million opportunities was first used by Motorola now being used worldwide by organizations.

The success of Motorola led IBM to adopt Six Sigma methodology which modified the MAIC and added Define to the process making it DMAIC. In 1989, Motorola made Six Sigma its flagship methodology to quality and was followed by GE, Kodak, and Xerox.

The concept has since then gained popularity around the world, and today it has become a standard to reach near-perfect products. The program from history has been adopted by well-recognized corporations like Kodak, IBM and Polaroid.

Progress of Shewhart, Ford, and Americans

The introduction of the assembly line and getting adopted by Henry Ford in the automobile industry made the dream of cost-effective mass production come true. The measurement of parts with standards was now becoming more accurate. The manual measurement was now reduced in contrast to going and no-go devices as it was being done before. The duty was now shifted to have consistent measurements according to the standards set so that the final products were in the quality's tolerance limits.

Another development was taken into account from statistical techniques called the sampling. The use of statistical tools in quality management were now becoming common.

In 1942, in such a rich climate for statistics Dr. Walter Shewhart, a statistician and an engineer, was brought to the Western Electric Company to enhance the quality of manufacturing procedures. Amongst the notable contributions of Shewhart, the first and foremost important contribution was the Process Control chart, which was to be spread across the quality management world in the coming decades.

By the 1930s, inspection officers or supervisors in American industries were moved from measurement and identifying defects in the process to define its stability. With higher volumes and complexity of parts being made industries were now dedicating a separate Quality Control Departments to the products.

WWII and growth in Japan

At the end of WWII, the Japanese were added by the American Forces under the leadership of MacArthur. The task was to help Japanese build from all the chaos MacArthur took services of W. Edwards Deming, a contemporary of Shewhart, to help in the reconstruction process. Deming pioneered the concept of PDCA (Plan-Do-Check-Act) cycle, which he named as Shewhart Cycle to Japanese manufacturers and provide training to the local engineers and managers in Statistical Process Control (SPC). The work of Deming in Japan laid the foundations for the decades to come and still his work is found in today Six Sigma Practices

An American Renaissance

At the beginning of the 1970s, the Japanese were more focused on quality even more than Americans. The Japanese businesses were following two practices defect elimination and reduction in production cycle's time.

The quality being offered by the Japanese manufacturer in automobile began to surpass that of American manufacturers as the Japanese automobiles were more efficient in fuel consumption when in 1973, the oil crisis hit.

US industry finally stood up and took notice. Juran and Deming, now with decades of experience in training for quality, were roped in to work a second miracle. Philip Crosby's book, "Quality is free", set out his 14-step approach to quality management and the principle of Zero Defects, which was eventually discarded and largely ignored on account of being absolutist and impracticable.

Taking notes from both sides of the developed world the Geneva-based International Standards Organization presented a quality standard in 1987, made after the old British BS 5750 system 1901, the new system was called ISO: 9000.

The idea was to make sure that the production stays uniform and quality management has a set of practices and guidelines to follow. The ISO, however, confirms the consistency of manufacturing and production procedures and not of the final product being made.

Japanese Contributions to American and European Industries

The contribution of the Japanese in quality management is at a broader spectrum. Japanese quality teams like the ones working for Toyota, an auto giant, came up with a lot of methodologies and ideas which were absorbed in the Six Sigma making like Toyota's Kanban squares, Just-In-Time manufacturing, Kaizen, Quality Circles, etc.

A lot of the concepts were used up by the European and American industries, few of them were at first dismissed due to being "culturally unadoptable" like the Total Quality Management. Later on, the cultural differences were let go and they were adopted to provide better manufacturing.

A Contribution from General Electric to Six Sigma

The General Electric, however, is considered to be the one to boost its present popularity and prominence.

General Electric introduced the three elements of the Six Sigma approach:

Delighting customers

- Making sure customers are setting standards for the business rather than a manager from within a company
- Putting a deep focus on the company's delivery, price, performance, reliability, transaction processing, and service.

Outside-in Thinking

- The company is being seen from the perspective of the customer
- The behavior or feeling of the customer towards the processing of the business
- Knowledge or comments from the customers are used to improve the company's processing and to add value to business

Leadership Commitment

- GE realized that in order to create profit and results people/employees are the key
- Providing employees with opportunities to develop themselves in providing services which will bring customers
- Making sure that the employees are provided with the training they want

The steps taken by General Electric revolutionized the thinking of firms towards its company structure. Understanding the difference between making strategies and getting them implemented was much clear now.

Harry Mikel and The Six Sigma Academy

Harry Mikel, an ex-employee at Motorola, worked in collaboration with Richard Schroeder a colleague at Motorola and founder Six Sigma Academy back in the 1990s.

Like his quality management abstains, Mikel's goal was to educate and mentor employees with Six Sigma tools like Lean Six Sigma. He widened his approach in teaching and guiding business to successfully make use of Six Sigma principles in their organizations.

The first client of Mikel was Lawrence Bossidy of AlliedSignal, who implemented Six Sigma to turn his business around. Bossidy later on introduced Jack Welch, CEO of General Electric and a close friend of Bossidy, to the concept who made use of it at the company's wholesale and got a great deal of success from it. Some other notable clients of the Academy include Merrill Lynch and DuPont.

In 1987, Harry Mikel at Unisys got his inspiration from the Eastern martial arts to make use of the belt dialect to Six Sigma practitioners, hence labeling professionals with belts like Green Belt, Yellow Belt, Black Belt, and Master Black Belts.

Brief History of Lean Production

Since the past, Six Sigma improvement has proven to be an effective method to dominate the business world. Talking about the lean production revolution then it can be best understood from its history.

The idea of lean production originated from Japan and it is not something from the present time but it dates back to the 1900s. Japanese manufacturers were more focused on improving their production processes while maintaining quality. What Japanese were doing was, producing small batches of products instead of mass production with continuous improvement to process and quality called Kaizen.

Kaizen and Lean production

Kaizen is a Japanese word meaning "change for better". In 1950, Toyota made use of the technique in its production process for better productivity, technology, quality and safety measures. The inclusion of Kaizen in Toyota came to be known as the "Toyota Production System".

The idea behind kaizen was that small continuous improvements to the system lead to larger changes and hence transformations take place. The western countries were thrilled by the idea and have been effectively using the method in their processes to this very day.

The change in customer requirements

The customers, however, were well satisfied with products that got inspected after being produced rather than products inspected during the production. This phenomenon of after development inspection was known as quality control where the products were inspected after they were made. However, the quality control products satisfied the customer for a long period of time.

Inspection is a costly procedure that doesn't add up to the quality of the product. Relying alone on inspection can't improve the production process. Inspection as a quality control fails to stop defected products from being produced with higher chances of having a human error in the process.

A brief history of Kaizen

Since the twentieth century, achieving the production of higher quality products has been the main concern for businesses.

Kaizen was born after the end of World War II when American occupation forces were assigned to help the Japanese recover from the war. In the process, Japanese business managers along with American experts created new ways to improve quality and processes.

Saki chi Toyoda, founder of Toyota Industries Co. Ltd., is the leading inventor of the process leading to the "Toyota Production System". The production system was adopted by various Japanese manufacturers to include small continuous improvement in their procedures.

The Kaizen Revolution

Before 1986, western countries weren't introduced to kaizen concept and Japanese manufacturers were considered as most efficient in the world.

In today's world, kaizen is used side by side with Lean Six Sigma by manufacturers across the globe. The idea of continuous improvement challenges industries to perform better than before and encourages innovation.

Kaizen segregates the different business processes and inspects each one of them while limiting the number of errors and reducing wastage. A great benefit of kaizen is that it identifies the problem at an early stage so that it can be solved prematurely.

Kaizen revolves around the concept that neglected small errors in the system can build up to be a major hazard for the business process at a later stage. Kaizen, when implemented to every minor area of the business, leads to achieving overall perfection in the system as each day passes by.

The continuous improvement and kaizen have originated a combined concept for the American and Japanese manufacturers. Both nations have been at the very front of this development.

Quality circles a part of Kaizen

One of the processes of continuous improvement is Quality Circles. Quality circles can be defined as gathering up a team of workers to discuss the quality of the product being made.

Generally, in quality circles workers from different levels i.e. strategic, managerial, bottom line supervisors gather up for a meeting on a regular basis. The meetings are called after a specific interval of time usually after every three months.

In quality circles, suggestions are highly appreciated on how to improve or modify the product and how to bring change to the working practices and processes. The members of the meeting are required to portray the issue in a logical manner.

Issues of the wider spectrum are also discussed as it is believed that it will ultimately affect the environment. In a few organizations, the quality circles are implemented in the fields of health and safety, training and education, and employee benefits and bonuses programs. Quality circles in organizations are encouraged by:

- Rewarding the members of circles from the company's profit earned
- Allotting a separate budget for such meetings, making sure management is attentive of the issues being discussed
- Providing feedback to employees why their suggestions got rejected and management asking comments and suggestions on specific problems and issues

The concept of quality circles has been accepted at such a broader scale that groups are drawn from separate organizations having a common interest to discuss.

Following quality circles is a part of continuous improvement which can be taken into account as the initiation of lean production.

Pillars of the Toyota Production System

Lean production methodology also known as Toyota Production System follows the ideology of "to get the right things to the right place at the right time".

The Toyota Production Systems stands on two pillars Kaizen and Genchi Genbutsu. Kaizen follows the concept of continuous improvement and takes it as a challenge, while Genchi Genbutsu is the respect for the people which grips teamwork and respect.

Lean production is a philosophy that targets minimal use of resource including time. The process identifies and eliminates all non-value addition actions.

Taiichi Ohno, an engineer is considered a pioneer in developing lean production principles. He claimed that the process eliminated waste and provided better production flow and better quality.

Lean production core principles

Lean process improvement or Lean production has an organized waste elimination system like:

- Early production and overproduction, which is to produce according to the demand of the customers
- Waiting, any time delay which is not adding value to the product or idle time
- Transportation, not being able to handle the supply of materials
- Inventory, unnecessary purchase or holding of raw materials
- Motion, works or machine not having the proper actions and not adding value to the product
- Over-processing, adding unnecessary steps or procedures which are wasting time
- Defective units, production of a component which needs fixing or is scrap

Researches have shown that lean production reduces the response time of production systems so that it can meet with a rapid change of market demands.

Roots of Lean Production

In the 1980s, lean process improvement was adopted by many European and US manufacturers giving different levels of success.

In recent years, greater interest in lean production has been shown by manufacturers, especially, when it comes to waste reduction. Boeing Aircraft and Dell Computers have adopted the lean production idea with great success.

Lean process improvement is not limited to manufacturing only, but it has shown great success in the service environment as well. Every system no matter which type has some waste i.e. something that doesn't add value to the product or customer.

The 5Ss of Lean improvement system

The 5Ss comes under lean production which further refines the idea of Lean production. The 5Ss follow the ideology that "there is a place for everything and everything goes in its place". Pride, simplicity, standardization, discipline, and repeatability are stressed in the 5Ss as being serious to efficiency.

| **Seiri or Structurize** | Discard or Segregate, i.e. introduce order where possible |
| **Selton or System** | Identify and Arrange for usage ease, i.e. |

	approaching tasks in a systematic order
Seiso or Sanitize	Clean daily, i.e. avoid clutter
Seiketsu or Standardize	Go through each 'S' every now and then, i.e. be consistent in approach
Shitsuke or Self-Discipline	Be motivated, i.e. follow the above 'S' daily

Comparing Lean And Six Sigma

One of the most discussed topics in the business world is the difference between Lean and Six Sigma. A great many people have solid sentiments about which technique is increasingly compelling for reducing expenses and killing waste. It is about personal favors and also about which technique has suited their business the most.

Lean assembling is a methodical approach for reducing waste and making stream in the creation process if we define it simply. On the other hand, Six Sigma is about a set of strategies that endeavor to significantly lower the pace of deformities. Basically, it reduces the defect overall.

Both Lean and Six Sigma have similar objectives if we see superficially. The two of them look to wipe out waste efficiently and make the most proficient system to conduct any process. However, they adopt various strategies on how to overcome certain problems and accomplish a target.

In the least difficult terms, the principle contrast among Lean and Six Sigma is that they spot the waste in a process using different methodologies.

One can say that the central difference between them both is that Six Sigma is a program while the Lean is the philosophy.

When Lean Stands Alone

The activity or the need for a process is the first thing that is considered under Lean. If the activity turns out to enhance the value, then Lean creates a better process flow to increase and improve the outcome. Lean works by removing any function or activity that is not valuable – in the Lean term, it is considered as a waste and needs to be removed from the system. Simply, it could be said that any item in the process that does not include the significant worth should be eliminated.

Lean is a ceaseless and on-going approach under the belief that everyday changes in innovation, outside conditions, and different factors will always leave opportunities to get better. As the name proposes, it separates processes to the exposed bone under its core value.

Lean goes for non-stop improvement over the whole esteemed stream of tasks by empowering the whole workforce to recognize and kill waste in their area. It is an on-going process instilled in the tasks of the firm and requires appropriation by the whole workforce in all parts of the organization activities for viability.

When Six Sigma Stands Alone

Six Sigma focuses on removing the process differences in output without emphasizing much on the importance of such a process. Here, Six Sigma doesn't ask questions related to the value that a function or activity might add. Instead, it considers all the variations as waste. Six Sigma is a task-based approach. It does not address whether any movement or capacity causes more value.

A significant distinction between Lean and Six Sigma relates to the responsibility for ideas cause more value. It just works under the core value that any variation in the existing process or yield is squandered. It centers explicitly around disposing of process varieties without investigating the benefits of such process in the plan itself.

Key Differences Between Lean and Six Sigma

The following are the major differences between lean and six sigma

Here are the most significant difference between Lean and Six Sigma:

- The fundamental idea of Lean belief is the expulsion of waste while Six Sigma is focused on the disposal of variations in processes.

- Lean is characterized as an efficient method for removing waste from the frameworks of an organization. The Six Sigma alludes to a process where a predetermined quality is kept up in the item by following certain means toward that path.

- The execution of Lean will bring about consistency in the results of a process. On the other hand, Six Sigma strategies will prompt the decrease of the flow time of the tasks.

- The point of Lean is to enhance productivity by expanding efficiency while Six Sigma targets satisfying customer's necessities.

- Lean uses visual tools, conversely, Six Sigma relies on pure science and insights.

- The Lean was created by Toyota while Motorola presented Six Sigma.

- Lean is centered on the flow mainly and Six Sigma is issue centered.

Lean and Six Sigma as Lean Six Sigma

Lean and Six Sigma are now being used together as one process for improving the process by removing waste strategically alongside lowering process variation. When both are combined together they focused on eliminating the eight kinds of waste that are renowned as muda in the business world. Formerly, Lean and Six Sigma were used separately, but the first time the concept of Lean Six Sigma was created in 2001 in a book by Barbara Wheat, Mike Carnell, and Chuck Mills. Since then, they are being used side by side because of the benefits they offer.

DMAIC is used in Lean Six Sigma like Six Sigma. When working together, Six Sigma is used to lower defects while Lean leads to the elimination of waste. Lean Six Sigma uses the tools and methods of both Lean and Six Sigma to gain the desired outcomes. Like judo, their masters are designated as master black belts, green belts, yellow belts, and white belts. For every belt, there's a specific set of skills.

Lean and Six Sigma are organized by Lean Six Sigma in lowering the production cost while improving quality. Also, it helps in enhancing the pace of the process by staying competitive in the market. Using both together also ensures saving the revenue to much extent; lean helps in this matter by reducing the amount of waste in the process while Six Sigma reduces variation in a process.

Lean and Six Sigma when make Lean Six Sigma provides a well-balanced relation that not only leads to money-saving but also improves the manufacturing process of a product or a service overall.

Chapter II: Being Open to Change as a Business

Working with Ideas

An idea can be a spontaneous thought in the mind that can do wonders for any individual. However, in the business world, an idea is considered a leap when it is a success. An idea in the business world carries a higher risk, as a single mistake can make the whole structure fall. Working carefully with precautions and taking a calculated plan of action is a necessity. Entrepreneurs are always on the urge of implementing great ideas and skyrocketing their business from ground level to sky-high.

Coming with a solid idea in the business world can be quite challenging, as every action must only be performed after calculating its outcome. Knowing what you are working for and staying motivated along the way is important. A single diversion from the goal can cause mayhem and leave all your effort to go to waste.

Before taking action, consider taking sound data into account then work accordingly. Without data you are left with opinions, however, with data, your answers are free from emotions and promote acceptance.

An idea can be for a small business and not necessarily for a corporation. Understand first that a company is a mixture of different projects that are being worked together, while a small business handles one project at a time. For this reason, Six Sigma can also be integrated with a small business. A big company will be able to implement Six Sigma multiple times while a small business will only be able to implement it once as they are on a smaller budget and can't bear project loses.

Treating Customer the Right Way

Understand the concept of having an idea with the example below:

Consider yourself an owner of a hair salon and you are always available at the front desk. You charge $30 for hair cutting. Now a new customer walks in, not aware of your service charges. He starts the conversation like this:

Customer: I have a budget of $20 can I get a haircut?

You: Ah sorry, we don't provide haircutting services at that budget.

Now the above conversation seems like the day to day conversation - you saying no to the customer with a lower budget could be a norm. There is nothing wrong with saying no but it could have been said differently. What you have lost here is a customer for life with very little charges to ever come again and ask you.

Here is what you could have said instead of saying the above statement.

Customer: I have a budget of $20, can I get a haircut?

You: Sorry, sir/ma'am we can't provide you a haircut in $20, what we can do is recommend you some hair salons nearby who will definitely provide a haircut within that budget. So may I recommend some?

Notice that both the statements are simply saying no to the customer. However, the second statement sounds more professional and posing an image on the customer that you are willing to help them with their problem.

After that, you can also do one more thing here. If you offer a trimming service, for example, in the customer's budget, you can say that you give this service in the given budget. You can further politely ask whether they are interested in it? Your first approach to help might change the customer's mind of complete hair cut and he/she might settle with only a bit of hair trimming today.

Common Mistakes of Businesses

The biggest mistake made by any business makes is turning a customer down without showing eagerness to solve their problem. A simple solution can do wonders for a business in a customer's eyes. Businesses failing to understand that is simply ignorant of what they are losing gradually.

Hospitality doesn't cost much but sure leaves a mark on a customer. Remember, every time it is the customer that pays for the goods or services so he has some expectations and a level of satisfaction that he needs to fill.

A small business with minimum items can have a greater turnover in a day than a business having multiple items to serve and all of that is because of treating customers the right way.

How Small Businesses can benefit from Six Sigma

Six sigma approach is more towards customer satisfaction than the enterprise's processing method. Any business can be run with Six Sigma as it is more project-focused than the size of the business.

Every single business project can be implemented with Six Sigma. The key is to sale what you advertise, a lot of times a customer is attracted by an ad campaign but it turns out that reality differs from what was shown. Such incidents lead to a bad reputation and reduce the chances of gaining any trust from the customer's friend circle.

Six Sigma can be implemented in business by eliminating all necessary steps from production and saving time in processing. Working according to the need of the customer can be the very first step. Eliminate the need of your customers and understand their needs according to their problem. A simple solution to the customer will be much appreciated and they are likely to return to your business for the next time they have a problem.

What Business Can you Run with Six Sigma

Consider yourself a business manufacturing smartphones, instead of providing your customers with premade cell phones you can give them the luxury of custom build smartphones. How that is going to work? Well, you start with some basics like shape, size, and design.

- You can provide the option of smartphone bodies with unique rigid edges. The edges can be diamond cut, rounded, etc.

- Next, allow the color palette to customers to make the color of their choice for the smartphone.

- For the design, you can have options like how many buttons the customers want on their phone. Do they desire a single button, three buttons, two buttons, etc. Give them the choice if they want their screen panel to be a touch screen or have a fingerprint sensor. Allow the variation for different unlocking sensors like fingerprint, face recognition, retina recognition, etc.

- For the specifications, you can have custom specifications like 4 GB RAM with 64 GB ROM with a 3.0 Quad-Core processor, or you can allow the choice of choosing Ram, Rom and processor according to the need.

- For the mobile casings provide the option of metal to wood to plastic whatever the customer likes.

- Let the customer chose the level of screen protection from durable to average and many other things regarding how they want their cell phones.

- The most important thing that will come is the price of the phone make it affordable yet versatile, which can be done by finding cheap labor markets and reasonable parts market.

- Allow the option of premium option for wealthy customers, so they can buy accordingly. For the customers with a tight budget make the custom phone as near as possible to the price in the market of the mobile having the same specifications. Or you can simply target the elite class for custom mobile options which will decrease your buyer's market.

- Make smartphones with accuracy and according to the details of the customer. Keep a few samples for the customers to touch and feel the smartphone you are offering as they can know what you are providing is something of value.

Six Sigma Methodology and Culture for Organization's Benefit

What is Organizational Culture?

Organization culture, collectively, is the way how things are conducted by the members of any organization. It represents their common ways of communication and doing work. Organizational culture is a learned behavior, a discovered belief, developed by the group of people to deal with the troubles of internal integration and external adoption that has been taught to the newcomers. This culture has proven beneficial and considered as an ideal way to think and perceive within an organization.

These beliefs and values bring employees of any organization together. It opens the gateway to the success of the company and helps it attains its goals. In other words, it is the character of an organization – it defines the means by which things are conducted in any organization.

Organizational culture produces a limiting effect on the efficacy of the implementation of quality management. The policies and philosophies of any organization are designed while keeping in mind its organizational culture. Thus, to improve the performance of an organization that is favorable to all it is essential to adapt to the Six Sigma culture.

What is a Six Sigma Methodology and Culture?

The Six Sigma introduces a culture that leads to constant improvement by mainly two ways:

- Giving a deeper knowledge of processing and problem solving to the workers and management of an organization

- Changing the working process to make it more productive to gain better results

The Six Sigma culture is very different from the traditional cultures of any organization. In Six Sigma culture, not only people at senior and managerial posts are responsible for defining what improvements are needed, but it allows team members as well to suggest about it. State-of-art approaches and tools are used as an improvement method. It is all because, in Sig Sigma, improvement and process knowledge is widespread throughout and not restricted to a few people like in traditional culture.

Benefits of Using Lean Six Sigma Methodology and Culture

When Lean Six Sigma methodologies are applied correctly to all the processes used in an organization, it yields many benefits.

Who Gets the Benefit?

All associations, organizations, and people can enjoy the advantages of Lean Six Sigma, despite the industry, size, and nation of origin. No doubt, producers and manufacturers established the improvement strategies consistently in the past but the application that has changed the system came into existence a few decades ago.

The Six Sigma has the potential to totally reform the employees. It turns the passive employees of the company into active participants who can point out the problems and present the ways to solve them.

Customers gain the benefits as well since taking care of procedure issues always brings fewer deformities plus shorter lead times with improved experiences. Overall, we can say using this method benefits the manufacturers as well as customers.

How Does it Produce the Benefits?

Lean Six Sigma helps the organization to use its data strategically to eliminate defects. It allows enterprises to create a structure that improves the efficiency of the process to deliver better products. As Lean Six Sigma offers insight to discover the uncover problems and find their solutions, it benefits any organization in many ways.

By Increasing Profit

Lean Six Sigma positively impacts the profit of any organization by:

- Increasing the speed of producing goods and services: Reforming the techniques enhances the speed of the process and improving the quality side by side.

- Enhancing capacity: Improving the processing techniques lowers the workload on each unit thus increasing the capacity to produce more products or services.

- Using lesser resources: Improves the company's profit by producing more goods or services by using lesser resources.

Overall, Lean Six Sigma is beneficial for the profit and also the productivity of an organization. When used efficiently, it increases the company's revenue for the long term without compromising the quality of the product or services.

By Improving Efficiency

Lean Six Sigma Efficiently enhances the efficiency of the processes used in an organization by

- Making things adaptable: Developing easy to understand guidelines to improve work which leads to quicker business growth.
- Maintaining Important Assets: Recovering assets either income or materials from effective procedures enhances the availability of the resources to develop the business beyond.

By Decreasing Cost

One of the essential advantages is a decrease in expenses of the product or service related to enhancements of procedures. Lean Six Sigma lowers the cost of the products or services by:

- Managing time and productivity: Utilizing less time and diminishing deformities or blunders that can result in revisions are the two major objectives of using its methodology.

- Removing Extra process from processes: In manufacturing, every process might not be important, and pointing and removing that activity saves cost.

Understanding what customers exactly look up to and finding a way to wipe out redundant steps while expanding value, organizations utilizing Lean Six Sigma methodologies recognize that they can essentially lower costs while improving and enhancing customer satisfaction.

By Enhancing Effectiveness

Lean Six Sigma enhances the effectiveness of any organization by:

- Defining and recognizing customers' prerequisites: It empowers the organization to focus its endeavors to lead them where they have the most value by understanding the customers and their imperatives.

- Improving Customer value: Estimating what customers are actually looking for causes the organizations to target improved activities to enhance their experience even further.

Lean Six Sigma assists organizations in the production of proficient and viable procedures. Accomplishing operational achievements enable the company to provide better services and products to the growing customers and make them even more satisfied.

By Developing Efficient Team

Lean Six Sigma builds up a framework to have an efficient team by:

- Relying on workers to run reformed endeavors: Group members are glad to claim procedure changes. Connecting the team to critical thinking and problem-solving techniques makes the groups accountable to one another and their company.
- Building reliance: Straightforwardness through all degrees of the organization advances respect and common comprehension of how every individual is a part of the hierarchical achievement.

- Improving employees' efficiency: Creating a sense of ownership in the employees makes them accountable to each other.

Training employees by making them learn important aspects of Lean Six Sigma makes them efficient team members who can constantly combat the problems that occur during a production process.

By Increasing Customer Satisfaction

Lean Six Sigma procedures mainly focus on the demands and needs of the customers. It increases customer satisfaction by:

- Making customers loyal: Organizations will undeniably bond to get repeated business if customers' requirements of quality are constantly fulfilled. Since consistency in quality is something the consumers take note of, it gives the surety of improved business.

- Satisfying customers: The better the item or administration, the more joyful the customers will be. Lean Six Sigma enables organizations to improve procedures and quality control which leads to superior services and products in the term of quality and value.

This strategy supports consumer loyalty and satisfaction by giving greater importance to customers. Lean Six Sigma centers on the improvement of the products, in addition to enhancements of product delivering techniques. It also augments actions related to customer service that further perks up the customer's contentment.

Lean Six Sigma, when adapted by the organization in the correct manner, contributes to the progression of it. Also, when it becomes a culture to follow in any company, it takes everyone associated towards betterment. Leaders of the company first need to understand this culture fully so that it could run in every sector of the organization gradually.

Tips for Implementing Lean Six Sigma

Six Sigma techniques are being used all over the world because of the benefits they provide to the organizations. In the business world, these methodologies are helping to achieve the organization's goals that were impossible to attain without their presence.

When an organization decides to adopt Six Sigma, it becomes essential for it to makes its implementation as successful as possible. There are many things to look for. There are many things that an organization must consider; here are the top tips for implementing Lean Six Sigma methodologies and culture:

The change should be made in Attitude

The experienced people in the industry think the transition in attitude is necessary to bring a significant change while adopting Lean Six Sigma techniques. Change in the process only will not suffice.

People tend to carry on with problems rather than solving them; it is a common attitude in any organization. That's where Lean Six Sigma comes beneficial and changes the behavioral aspects as well. It initiates the eagerness to frequently work out the hurdles in the business processes. When people are determined to reform their approach, the means of development will be implemented effortlessly. It leads an organization towards prosperity and creates a better working environment.

Training your employees about Lean Six Sigma methodologies is good, but without the attitude transformation, the whole exercise will be just theoretical without any practical outcome. It is necessary that it is considered as a behavioral approach, rather than just a process that is to follow. Certification will become vain when there is nothing practical at all.

The change of behavior should be considered as a tool for the successful implementation of Six Sigma and everyone needs to work for it. Lean Six Sigma should be adopted as an organizational culture not just as a tool for process improvement only.

Must be accepted as a part of the organization's core strategy

Including Lean Six Sigma in the company's main objectives and policies is the key feature for its rewarding implementation. Without this, the whole drive will be short-lived and people will reject the procedure long before it is properly developed in the organization.

When the organization's goals are different from that of the Lean Six Sigma, it becomes hard for the employees to adapt to the changes it brings. It makes them confused about what to do and what not, which many times, it makes the workers even lose faith in its effectiveness.

Furthermore, when an organization has basic procedures established at each base, incorporating Lean Six Sigma, it will increase the percentage of its triumph. When Lean Six Sigma methodologies are merged with the core strategies of the company, it becomes easy for everyone to go in the same direction. The Lean Six Sigma goals should match the organization's goals to gain the desired outcomes.

Must have a firm reason to adopt

Companies should have a firm policy or strong reason to adopt Lean Six Sigma. Having a strong motive behind adopting it is the first thing that makes it a success.

For example, the company that is facing many customer complaints regarding the quality of their products might need to implement Lean Six Sigma strategies in their business to improve the quality of their product. Another instance that could be considered is the company is having a difficult time completing the projects on time that is making others win their good market share.

Without having a firm stand, there is quite low encouragement to establish a continued progressive drive like Lean Six Sigma. Upper management and Leadership in a company should recognize strong reasons, and perceive how the process enhancement techniques like Lean Six Sigma can resolve the issues. When the goals are clear and the organization knows what it wants, the Six Sigma strategies help to achieve them faster.

But what happens when the company doesn't have a strong problem to solve? It is not always the case that without a firm stand and strong reasons Lean and Six Sigma cannot be enforced in any organization. Also, a strong motive behind the adaptation doesn't assure success. It is just that there will be more motivation for gaining big achievements to bring great benefits when a firm reason is present.

The approach must be top to bottom in the organization

Organizations across the globe may tend to implement Lean Six Sigma from low to high in their organizational chart. But industry professionals consider that engaging senior and middle managers first in process enhancement techniques have more beneficial effects. Their involvement in establishing Lean Six Sigma for developing crucial business methods will make connection behaviors strong thereby, increasing acceptance by others too.

Without the involvement of upper and middle managers, the prosperous implementation of Lean Six Sigma throughout the whole organization will be a tedious exercise. Managers play a better role here because they are in direct touch with the bottom line as well as higher leaderships. Workers usually tend to follow the example set by upper management. Thus, this approach becomes the best way to achieve goals.

It also becomes easy for an organization to complete its operations when the management knows what is happening and why it is happening.   As stated earlier that it must be adopted as a culture rather than a process to be effective so it should be adopted by all.

Must initiate with experts

Many times, establishing any new technique or a scheme's progress relay on how and with whom it begins. In companies around the globe, there will be some who are eager to try new things and finding ways to work than most of the people around. Instead of wasting your important time and strength on pessimists or non-believers, it is good to begin with only a few people who will lead the way and take up the task of establishing Lean Six Sigma. They can be the leaders and exhibit how it can improve their work. When people around them become inquisitive of their daily schedule, things will move toward positivity via the internal champion's web.

For Six Sigma implementation, the first choice matters the most because it is the process that makes things better from top to bottom. So initiating with the right people is suggested by the experts. Taking someone from outside is also helpful. There are many Six Sigma certified professionals ready to help you in this matter. When you gain the expert's recommendation for your processing and training, things eventually start to get better and you will be able to achieve your goals within your timeline.

Must select the right project

Selecting the right people to initiate with is not the only thing to look for – choosing the right project is also necessary. A few upper and middle managers, who can be leaders, won't be able to produce any fruitful results when a wrong project is selected. It will not be able to achieve the goals of the organization.

Indeed, you have to choose plans that are approved by upper and middle management that could produce fruitful results immediately. Selecting the right project leads to better results in the given timeframe. Also, it saves many resources that might have gone to waste with the wrong selection. When the desired results are achieved, it boosts the overall assurance in the Lean Six Sigma techniques by the employees. Success of one project will be welcomed by all and it becomes easy to generalized Six Sigma methodologies throughout the organization.

Must have a realistic approach in analyzing cultural differences

Every organization has its particular environment. Professionals consider that the working environment varies across geographical parts and various kinds of organizations. Different sectors like private, public, government, etc. have their own culture. They have their own ways to conduct any operation. The same could be seen as an individual. We all are different with our own traits, so are the organizations that we make.

When implementing the Lean Six Sigma,   it is good to skip making presumptions about how well it will produce its effects and what will be the results.

Considering the needs of the organization in this matter is beneficial. By doing this, it will be smooth adoption incorporation of Lean and Six Sigma techniques in an organization that will be beneficial for the organization as well as for its workers. Keeping in view the present culture of the organization yields fruitful results.

When the Six Sigma culture merges with the organizational culture, it becomes easy for the employees to accept it. Changing how an organization works take time but it is not possible specifically when this alteration leads towards betterment. Lean Six Sigma may induce its own culture but the results are beneficial for all at the end.

Must use the right measurement system

The first thing to consider here that only those things can be improved in an organization that can be measured. When you cannot measure, you cannot change according to Six Sigma. By adopting an appropriate assessment system, specialists can set benchmark criteria and utilize the information to make correct decisions. When individuals get the true strength of the Lean Six Sigma, there will be exponential progress in projects.

Right measurement tools can be used to clearly define what needs to be improved. The flaws of the system can be noted and the policies can be made to induce the change that will solve the issue. Also by supporting the individuals who understand and define all aspects of improvement, one can detect the developmental changes that have occurred and keep track of it.

The right measurements lead to gain the desired goals of the organization. But when the measurements are wrong, it becomes impossible to achieve the goals. One thing to make sure here is that measuring tools must also be evaluated every now and then in an organization because their mechanical error could impact the outcomes dramatically. Wrong results may fail Six Sigma in an organization and it may never be able to gain its benefit again.

Appropriate communication leads to success

A communication methodology manages a whole program or intervention. It establishes the direction and tone to achieve the desired change. Communication is always a two-way matter; when both sides are equally enthusiastic about the conversation, the better opinion could be achieved at the end.

A mere communication can never be enough in an organization. Having an open communication channel helps to obtain data and understand it for completing projects on time. For instance, sometimes a face-to-face talk or discussion is far more superior to some routine e-mails.

Considering the importance of communication, numerous organizations are already utilizing whiteboard displays with standard reports on work progress and visual outlines. It is one of the fail-proof strategies for better engagement with the audience. A communication in which the receiver will have an option to think and act on it produces better results.

The upper management usually communicates easily with the workers, but in turn, it is hard for the bottom line to approach them. So, to gain the Six Sigma benefit, it is better to listen to what workers say about the change. Your policy may improve drastically when everyone from top to bottom contribute their knowledge in it.

Must designs forums to maintain the progress in an organization

Knowledge management plays a key role in making the correct information available to the relevant people. It ensures that the organization proceeds to learn in the right direction. If needed. It will have the option to recover and utilize its knowledge assets in current applications and can be used again if required.

Another role of knowledge management is to support the advancement of basic business processes through Lean Six Sigma philosophies. It is valuable since it puts attention to information as a real resource. Practitioners of Lean and Six Sigma can gain a lot from each other's experience. It helps the firm to improve and center its knowledge development to match its needs.

Chapter III: Looking from Customers Perspective

Understanding Customer Needs

Before understanding the needs of the customer, it is important to understand why is it a necessity? Business gets its success or failure due to its customers. One way or another a business gets its name on the lists of the customer, however, it can be a positive one or a negative one.

The quickest way to gain positive feedback from multiple customers is to just treat the very first customer with care and respect. Once that is done the word of mouth from your very first customer will reach more people and the chain goes on and on. Marketing is something that creates a mutual relationship between a supplier and a customer.

The supplier might be giving goods or services and the right customer will consume according to his/her needs. The customer, however, isn't limited to only one role; a customer might have different roles. The roles can be of:

Buyer: The person who chooses a service or product

Payer: The person financing the purchase made

User: The person receiving the benefits of service or product

For example, a buyer could be the manager ordering the purchase of the coffee sachets. The payer is the finance department, paying for the coffee sachets. The users are those who have access to the coffee sachets.

The needs of any customer can be best understood once we understand how a customer behaves or the behavior of a consumer. The behavior of a consumer can be understood best with the help of how the marketers distinguish between each customer.

Buyer Behaviour

Taking buying behavior as a process makes it easy to differentiate between the different roles a customer takes. A marketer either takes consumers as buyers or organizations as buyers with both having a different demand.

Consumer as buyers

Consumer behavior can be divided into three main theories:

Cognitive Paradigm Sees buying as a result of rational decision making

Learned Behaviour Focuses on the past purchases made

Habitual Decision Making	Focuses on the habit and loyalty to a brand

A Consumer Decision Making Model

Lancaster and Withey defined that consumer decision making can be identified with five steps:

1. Recognizing need/problem
2. Searching information/pre-purchasing
3. Evaluation of substitutes
4. Decision for purchasing
5. Post-purchase evaluation

Element	Remark
Recognizing need/ problem	A customer has identified a problem or needs to be solved. This can be used as a motive to search for a solution.
Searching information/pre-purchasing	Marketers can provide the product information, tailored according to need. The customer might pick a substitute.
Evaluation of substitutes	Marketers can offer a product for assessment and can give information

	about other products in the market.
Decision for purchasing	Making a choice and buying.
Post-purchase evaluation	The remarks of the customer, if they are dissatisfied they will back on recognizing need/problem. If they are satisfied the process will be cut short and they will shift to the decision of purchasing and will be loyal to a brand.

This model is perfect for marketers to make use of as a framework. The description gives the idea about how to make use of every stage step by step.

What influences consumer buying behavior

Lancaster and Whitey defined some of the main influences of consumer buying behavior which can be divided as:

Influences on buyers

Social Factors

- Family
- Roles and status

- Reference groups

Cultural Factors

- Cultural
- Social class
- Sub-culture

Personal Factors

- Stage
- Economic
- Occupation
- Circumstances
- Age and life-cycle
- Lifestyle and Personality

Psychological Factors

- Learning
- Motivation
- Perception
- Beliefs and Attitudes

Social factors

A person is affected by the society he lives in or the social grouping trends which influence his/her buying behavior. Understanding of consumer occupational roles, gender-related is socialization examples.

A role is a system or sum expectations that are expected from an individual. Take a man, for example, a male might be a husband or a father, a good neighbor, a supporter and an active member of community and sports club, a professional or even a tradesman.

A reference group can be something out of imagination or might an actual group which has an impact on a person's desires or behavioral evaluations. The reference group rises the sense of comparison in an individual that what he/she is buying in comparison to the group, subconsciously building an individual's attitude with the group.

A family varies in many different ways, not only in a wider subject of socio-economic status but in consumption patterns and in buyer behavior.

Cultural Factors

Culture includes the beliefs, attitudes, and values in the life of people who are interlinked together as a member of society. Culture includes cultural lifestyles, artifacts, and so on. For example, alcohol consumption is part of western countries' culture but it has frowned in Muslim and other countries. Culture influences a lot more than other factors as it is part of the identity of an individual.

Personal Factors

Personal factors include factors like stage of family, life cycle, age, occupation, lifestyle, and economic circumstances.

The buying of an individual depends on his/her age. The products depending on age can be furniture, clothes, and recreation.

The family life cycle purchase behavior can be observed in the Western region. For example, a couple after marriage before having children will have different consumption patterns and needs than those couples whose children have left the house.

An occupation of a person will have an effect on a person's buying behavior and the marketers must identify the occupational groups having an above-average interest in their goods and services.

Buying patterns of an individual are also influenced by their economic circumstances which might be:

- Spendable income
- Assets and savings
- Borrowing power
- Spending vs. saving attitude

A lifestyle is how an individual lives a life which can be seen in their activities, interests, and opinions. Marketers must look for a relationship between their goods and different lifestyles. The lifestyle can, however, be divided into many classifications.

Psychological factors

Consumer buying behavior can be affected by four psychological factors:

1. Beliefs and attitudes
2. Motivation
3. Perception
4. Learning

Beliefs and attitudes

A belief is something a person holds within oneself. An attitude is a person's favorable or unfavorable assessment, emotional reaction, and action towards an idea or object. An attitude makes people behave constantly in the same way towards the same object. Attitudes are said to be inconsistent pattern change in one attitude majorly changes other attitudes.

Motivation

Motivation is defined as an inner state which activates or boosts, energizes or moves, channels or directs a person to do something.

- In 1954, Maslow gave a theory of motivation defining that people are compelled by "particular needs at particular times". Maslow claimed that human needs are set in a hierarchy according to their importance: social needs, self-actualization needs safety needs, psychological needs, and esteem needs.
- In 1968, Herzberg gave the "two-factor theory" of motivation that differentiates between the factors that cause dissatisfaction and factors that cause satisfaction.

Perception

Perception is a process where people choose, organize, and understand sensual incentives into a more refined logical picture. The view of a consumer varies due to interest, expectation, needs, past experience, attitudes and beliefs.

Learning

Learning is an outcome of events when an individual has learned something about a brand or product through past experience. The experience can be positive hence earning the loyalty of the customer or it can be negative which can result in losing a potential customer.

Consumers buying behavior is affected by multiple reasons. A consumer's loyalty can only be earned by understanding truly what a customer needs. Marketing to the right people at the right time can be a lot profitable than a campaign at the wrong time. For example, a large TV screen marketing campaign might do wonders right before the game season rather than a campaign being launched after the game season. Similarly, advertising Air Conditioners in the summertime will be a good idea than in winter.

What influences organization buying behavior

Organizations are considered to be more rational when it comes to buying than individuals. The buying behavior of a company is more formal than an individual. The buying behavior of a company is more out of a need than a want. The company purchases in order to further process it into goods.

When a consumer buys something it is known as Business to Consumer selling. While, when a business buys from another business it becomes business to business buying.

Thinking about selling to organizations then consider the following factors before getting started:

1. Organizational markets are limited and only have a few buyers, these few buyers are responsible for making much of sales.

2. The customer base of an organizational market is smaller and has greater importance and large buying power, making a close relationship between buyer and seller.

3. The industrial goods' demands are directly proportional to the demands of the consumers.

4. The buying decisions are made by a group of members and is not being made by a single person.

The buying process of an organization

Behavior	Statement
Stage 1: Understand the problem	The need to buy can be from within or outside the company.
Stage 2: Develop product accordingly to solve the problem	The buying decision is made by carefully understanding the problem and what can be done to resolve it.
Stage 3: Looking for products or suppliers to help with buying	The third phase of buying is equal to the information search of consumer behavior. This

	can include trade publications, supplier catalogs, trade publications, and asking proposals from suppliers.
Stage 4:Assessproducts according to the details	Such decisions are made to validate that the product being bought is according to the need of the production, service, price, and ability to deliver on time is considered crucial.
Stage 5: Choosing and ordering the most suitable product	The most suitable product is the one that is ordered from the right supplier. The order is placed by providing details about credit arrangements, deliver dates, technical assistant and terms set.
Stage 6: Assessing the product and performance of the supplier	The supplier is then assessed about the quality of the product provided and the supplier performing according to the terms of the contract.

How do organizations buy?

The biggest difference between an organization's and consumer's buying behavior is that buying decisions are hardly made by a single person. Commonly, in an organization, the decision is made by numerous people from various functional sectors having different designations within an organization. The group is called DMU (The Decision Making Unit).

Initiators: They are the ones who start the buying process and help express buying terms.

Influencers: They define the details and provide the possible substitutes available in the market.

Deciders: They are responsible for choosing the stated suppliers according to the requirements.

Approvers: Approve the proposals from buyers and deciders.

Buyers: They have the authority to choose the suppliers and negotiate the purchasing terms.

Gatekeepers: Have control over the flow of information and stop sellers from having access within the buying center.

Users: The end-user of the items bought.

The Decision Making Unit of a Company

The DMU isn't the same in every organization and varies from business to business. The structure, size, and formality of the DMU will differ depending on certain conditions. Key concerns include:

- Who are the main members of the buying process?
- In which sectors do they have the greatest influence?
- What is their influential level?

- On what basis do they evaluate as a member?
- How professionally is the buying process handled?
- To what measures are the buying centralized in bigger organizations?

The people in the buying process must be made sure that it is safe for them, they just have to make sure to handle it professionally. The process of organizational buying behavior differs at many different levels. In simple words, a consumer be buying behavior is quite simple and straight. While the buying behavior of an organization is quite complex and the purchasing has its own process like production. Companies believe in to buy the best product at the lowest price.

Customer needs vary from person to person. The satisfaction of customers varies from product to product. Every customer expects something from a seller and if that expectation is reached then the customer is happy. The chances of getting a loyal customer are by providing the level of satisfaction a customer desires.

Having a bad experience with a single customer can lead to permanent damaging results for a business. A business prospers on the way it treats its customers. The reputation of a business is what makes it successful, the higher the number of satisfied customers the more competitive it becomes to other businesses in the same field.

A lot of start-ups fail to understand the simple fact, the service isn't the only factor that affects a business' reputations the environment, staff, food everything comes into account. A business is more likely to find quick success if its objectives are in balance with customer needs.

Handling a customer's requirement profitably and efficiently is what is expected by the customer from a business.

Chapter IV: The Core Methodologies of Six Sigma

Core Principles of Lean Six Sigma

It is not always easy to determine what to improve even when the organization decides to do so. There are so many things to check and many issues to point. It is always hard to know how to start and where to start. The Six Sigma approach is considered to be the best in the world as it answers all these questions. Keeping in mind the core principles of Lean Six Sigma, one can directly head towards improvement.

The Lean Six Sigma covers each and every step of processing in a systemic manner – here are its core principles:

Giving priority to customers

It is the first principle is related to customers in Six Sigma as they hold much importance in its functioning. The business advice of the past is considered true today that a customer is always right. Customers play a key role in the success of any organization. They are necessary for any business to mature. Therefore, no matter what business you do, you should give the first priority to your customers always. Keep in mind that without fulfilling the demands of the customer, your business might stop to grow further.

Each choice you make ought to carry your organization closer to conveying the greatest esteem. It's a good pre-practice to be sure about maintaining the degree of quality you have guaranteed your clients before making any minor or intense changes. Your new process implementation should focus on your goals without affecting or only improving the quality of your product or service.

Improving the value of the customer is the key thing. Lean Six Sigma offers companies and individuals the core principles to drive the business forward, a holistic view for the whole business, not just one component of it. It defines your proper goals and tells you where you must stand. Like trying to optimize the production process of some items that no one likes, it carries almost no value in doing that, rather than advancing the production process of products that people enjoy and want the most.

The PDCA cycle or Deming Cycle could be used here. It checks out the six sigma idea of continuously improving the quality model. An unmistakable idea of what comprises quality in your business shapes how you are willing to improve items and processes. You have to comprehend what your worth is and how it can be further improved.

The model PDCA Cycle has four logical and continuous learning steps that include Plan, Do, Check, and Act. Sometimes, it is also referred to as the PDSA Cycle in which 'Check' is changed with 'Study'.

If you are evaluating the production and supply process, remove the steps which don't contribute much profit; using this practice you can comprehend what is inefficient and what is not. Of chance, if you do not evaluate then you just cannot viably figure out what is inefficient. Hence, you can not make changes to improve.

Process improvements lead to ending what is not important and not ending the process and customer value gives a clear picture of it.

Six Sigma focuses on understanding the needs of the customers by using all means. Changes should be made for improvement, but the quality should be sustained.

Understanding the heart of the process

Where your process is standing right now? Its evaluation is the only means to make the right decision and move forward. Designing of the value stream is what makes Lean Six Sigma special. It gives the complete idea of every step involved in your process and draws attention to the waste.

A couple of bits of plastic and glass on a mechanical production system, at last, become a LED TV? There is a value stream map for every progression that is involved in this process from buying all the necessary components, gathering them, running a quality inspection to dispersing the completed item. This stream map allows the organization to figure out which steps include more worth. Rest which does not work can be expelled from the procedure immediately.

Automated process mining is one of the core principles of Lean Six Sigma where whatever you do is process-driven. You can't simply leave things over a hunch, possibility, or any capacity because a process should be all smooth and practical.

All things considered, one of the initial steps is to make sense of and comprehend the issues.

The bottleneck seems to be the common and most clear inability to accomplish a smooth process stream. It is a zone of the process that is performed below the standard. It brings all levels down depending on it to its own level or the opposite of it where a zone of the process has the capability to perform far more than other levels.

When process mining is used during any process, programmed software is used according to the user's need; it can call attention to most bottlenecks as a feature of its analysis. Automated Business Process Discovery (ABPD) tools, in general, have the ability to recognize bottlenecks and bring them to light.

You can generally use the strategy of 5 whys to figure out the root cause. Usually, when the problem occurs, it is due to the malfunctioning of the system or when any process is lacking. The 5 whys are for only small operations. Here is one example that might help you – it is the example of your car stopped on a road.

- Why did the car stop? (First why) – The engine has seized.

- Why did the engine seize? (Second why) - There was insufficient lubrication inside the engine, it locked the crankshaft.

- Why was there insufficient lubrication? (Third why) – The oil pump on the engine is not circulating enough oil inside.

- Why is the pump not circulating enough oil? (Fourth why) – the pump intake is clogged with metal shavings.

- Why is the intake clogged with metal shavings? (Fifth why, a root cause) – Because there is no filter on the pump.

Using five whys technique lead to the root cause of the issue which can be solved using Six Sigma strategies.

Eliminating waste without compromising quality

When you have assembled your present value stream, you can distinguish issues with your work and tackle them. Remove activities that have no value at all. Lean Six Sigma philosophy is tied in with finding where issues emerge, fixing them, and averting future events. There is no need to showcase the sectors that are working flawlessly as it will diverge the attention from the main problem. Though it will make your employees happy to see the progress, but it is better to remain focused.

In an event where your value stream guide does not explain precisely where the issue lies, you can use a few different approaches, like logical result graphs, cause and effect graphs also called the fishbone diagram and any other statical method. They can assist you to look at another angle to find the root cause. Affinity diagram could also come in handy; you can brainstorm issues with it by taking help from the involved group to make things fast and more effective.

Anything that does not contribute towards production is a waste. Remove it out in order to prioritize the company's value.

Focusing on eliminating waste is called "Muda" within a manufacturing system. It is a Japanese word meaning uselessness or wastefulness. It is the basic concept of Toyota Production System (TPS); it gives insight on each level of production from raw materials to resources needed to mold materials into a complete product and improves overall revenue.

Under the TPS, seven basic Muda are identified as:

1. Overpopulation (waste)

2. Inventory (waste)

3. Transportation (waste)

4. Defected stock (waste)

5. Over-processing (waste)

6. Waiting (waste)

7. Motion (waste)

Understanding the 7 Muda is easy but figuring out how to get rid of them as much as possible is a difficult job. Here are a few tips that are presented to eliminate waste for each Muda.

1- Overpopulation - Synchronize processes. Man and machine should work accordingly.

2- Inventory - Measure the waste and keep raw material and finished goods inventories clean.

3- Transportation - Utilize the most straightforward routes to reach a destination.

4- Defected stock - Be accountable, develop a system for quality assurance.

5- Over-processing - Get customers' standards and expectations on time.

6- Waiting - Be conscious, increase the reliability of processes.

7- Motion - Reduce travel time between stations. Decrease unnecessary machine movements.

When a specific classification of waste is identified, it's conceivable to execute techniques that will handle specifically that waste. The same goes for another Muda. Once it's identified which sector in the organization produces which sort of waste, you can take countermeasures to get the quantity of waste to near zero.

For example, you can counter waste overproduction through synchronizing processes (Man and machine). When things are accordingly, production will go smoothly with almost no waste. Or it can be encountered with Lean manufacturing techniques. On the other hand, One Piece Flow Assembly systems can be used to counter waste excess processing itself.

Having a smooth workflow

Nothing is going to change unless you take the first step. Make up your mind on how you want to fix or improve things, go for it. It's like the law of inertia. If a ball is rolling, it will continue to roll unless friction or some other force stops it. A body in motion tends to stay in motion and a body at rest tends to stay at rest. The same goes for any organization or company or even an individual. Nothing is going to change unless you induce a change.

Labor will continue to work or not work; they will continue the similar undertakings until someone from the management chooses something else for them.

Convey new guidelines and practices to follow if you want the change. Be certain that every representative or worker gets proper training and look out for criticism. Otherwise, the problem will not be solved.

Lucidchart can be used to create a simple process map to convey to your workers what's new about their work process. Knowing about the change and its results can work like a force that will keep them motivated in doing the work.

The work must go smoothly. The obstacles should be managed beforehand to gain the best results.

Make the change acceptable throughout

Lean Six Sigma requires a ton of progress and change. You have to welcome a change and ask your workers and labor to accept it too. If you'll put yourself in your labor shoes' you might fear or panic by hearing the news of change. As so much of work is now computerized, it could result in losing their job. Make things clearer from your end on how these computerized operations will help workers in making things much easier. Show them how convenient you have made their work.

As a major aspect of this move, your organization should consistently search for better approaches to streamline the process and counter waste. Watch out the data, examine it, and regulate your procedures where important.

Although directors and experts can settle on astounding choices looking down the workflow from where they stand, labor or workers involved are not behind. In each step, they might have a better understanding and significant knowledge as well because they are the ones doing the job.

The fact of the matter is, workers who are involved in the processes every day might have a useful opinion that would, in fact, result in product improvement. They know about machines and resources very well because they deal with them daily. Their contribution can improve the process and guarantee the company's growth. This is the approach adopted by Toyota.

It tells to go and see the work where it is actually happening as nothing can provide process details better than that.

Inside Six Sigma, various individuals from different teams liable for the improvement task are given titles:

- Process owner

- Process champion

- Black belt

- Green belts

All these titles have various duties, some of which can be about engaging with other staff and convey messages to representatives. Getting different groups in the organization to perceive the issue and to make arrangements to solve is an important aspect of Six Sigma job.

Including staff in the improvement process is the best way to approach a problem and to solve it. Running an association is not like coding a personal computer. People are included, you have to make things easier for labor to ensure the process runs smoothly. Six Sigma focuses on the team that is not burdened but relaxed while producing the top quality results.

Having a systematic and scientific approach

On a basic level, the motivation behind why Six Sigma is so popular approach is that it defines a framework through which your company can improve its processes. It's the era of information; Six Sigma has a logical quality that takes advantage of the information drive world. It only seems fair to take the benefit of the collected data and use it for making enhancements and improve further processes through it

This same feeling goes right back to masterminds like Frederick Winslow Taylor and W. Edwards Deming who in real launched a logical way to deal with business tasks.

Ideas like the TPS are originated from Japanese culture with Deming being one of the minds behind it. He went to Japan after the 2nd world war and is credited with the process improvement of Japans' post-war interests.

One aspect of Six Sigma is using a scientific approach to achieve results is present in the form of the DMAIC process. It tells how to define the problem and measure the success rate even before the initiation of the process.

Understanding what is DMAIC?

DMAIC is a strategy to implement Six Sigma into a business. DMAIC stands for:

Define

Measure

Analyze

Improve

Control

It is a five-phase strategy that leads to solutions to the problems of unknown causes.

Define means to know the problem that is in need of fixing? Define means to get answers to some of the questions like defining:

- Who are the customers?
- What are their needs according to the product or service?
- What is the initiation point of the process of the problem?
- What is the finishing point of the problem?
- When will the problem be considered solved?
- In what direction and flow will the process flow?

Understanding the voice of the customer is important. Once understanding the need of the customer the team can then move to the next step of the DMAIC for further processing.

Measure means to know how the process is currently flowing. Measure means to collect data from:

- Multiple sources to know the defect and metric types.
- Comparison of customer surveys to know what is lacking?

Analyze means to make use of data collected from measure to determine the possible defects and how to solve them. Look into matters like:

- Identify gaps between the current process and the object to reach
- Know the different types of sources from where the data was collected
- Make room for opportunities for overall improvement

This is the most crucial part of the process as analyzing the root cause of the problem is very important. Failing to come up with root cause makes the process even more complicated and teams find it impossible to provide a solution to the customer's problem.

Jumping to conclusions without proper leaves a big question mark the whole time for the customer and the team solving the problem. No matter how many methods are implemented the solution doesn't seem to arrive.

Improve means to modify the secondary process by providing a creative solution to solving and preventing problems

- Make creative solutions to solve the problem
- Make and set up implementation plans

To improve is to refine the overall structure of the solution process here is the part where teams get to know the core reason for the problem and make it easy to counter it.

Control means to keep the improvements merged with the new process. Keeping the new processed maintained is demanded from the team and it does so by monitoring the plan to track the plan's success. Once the process is considered a true success the current process is updated to the best solution available.

The systems and structures are modified to the latest solution and are referred first to the future problems. The 5Ss are used to keep the process at its most efficient level.

Tools used in DMAIC

DMAIC stands for Define, Measure, Analyze, Improve and Control. The DMAIC comes under the methodology of implementing Six Sigma. Knowing what tools can be used in the five phases of DMAIC makes it easy to implement the methodology.

Define

Define phase can be used in a step by step process:

- Describe the problem by building a Problem Statement
- Describe the objective or goal by making a Goal Statement

- Describe the process using Process Map
- Describe types of customers and what they need
- Make it clear to others involved in the Project process

The following tools can be used in Define phase to outline the steps:

- A3
- Swim lane Map
- Tree Diagram
- Project Charter
- Relationship Map
- Value-stream Map
- Voice of the Customer Translation Matrix
- SIPOC (Supplier, Inputs, Process, Outputs, Customers)

Measure

Measure phase can be used in a step by step process:

- Know the current state of the process
- Build a plan on collecting data
- Make sure data is from a reliable source
- Collect the data from point zero
- Modify the project charter

The following tools can be used in the Measure phase to outline the steps:

- Check sheets
- Project charter
- Data collection plan
- Operational Definitions

Analyze

Analyze phase can be used in a step by step process

- Carefully observe the process
- Display the data collected in graphical form
- Look for the root cause of the problem
- Verify the reason(s) the problem occurs
- Modify the project charter

The following tools can be used in the Analyze phase to outline the steps:

- 5 Whys
- Box Plots
- Run Charts
- Histograms
- Pareto Charts
- Project Charter
- Fishbone Diagram
- Value Stream Map
- Root Cause Hypothesis

Improve

Improve phase can be used in a step by step process

- Brainstorm the possible solutions to fix the problem
- Select the solution which is practically implementable
- Develop Maps of Process depending upon the various solutions
- Choose the best solution(s)

- Apply the Solution(s)
- Measure to make sure there is an improvement

The following tools can be used in the Improve phase to outline the steps:

- To-Be Map
- PDCA/PDSA
- Plot Checklist
- Benchmarking
- Brainstorming
- Swim Lane Map
- Value Stream Map
- Impact Effort Matrix
- Implementation Plan
- Weighted Criteria Matrix
- Classic Lean Improvements

Control

Control phase can be used in a step by step process

- Make sure the process is properly monitored and managed
- Make the document of improved process
- Make modifications to other sectors
- Celebrate and share your success
- Make continuous improvements to the process using Lean production principles

The following tools can be used in the Control phase to outline the steps:

- Control Plan
- Gallery Walks
- Control Charts

- Documentation
- Monitoring and Response plan
- Innovation Transfer Opportunities

Understanding what is DMADV?

DMADV is a strategy to implement Six Sigma into a business. DMADV stands for:

Define

Measure

Analyze

Design

Verify

The DMADV should be used when there is a need for developing a non-existent product at the factory. Or when a product is already being made at the factory but needs to be up to the customer's specification or Six Sigma Methodology.

The five phases of the DMADV are defined below:

In the **D**efine phase, the basic reason for the project is defined or the purpose of the project is understood. Once the reason is known then realistic and measurable goals are seen from the view of the company. The steps are developed about how to tackle the situation and what could be the risks. A clear understanding of the goal is set during this phase and is set according to the company's and customer's specifications.

In the Measure phase, the necessary factors to quality are measures. The steps must be considered are: understanding the needs and market sector, knowing the crucial design restrictions, recalculating the risk and understanding the capability of production procedure, making scorecards that will align the design parts more crucial to quality. Once all the aspects are understood then a calculative method can be made to begin the production.

In the **A**nalyse phase, the alternatives to designs are developed, conceptual designs are developed, the best parts for the designs are evaluated, and the best design is developed. The total cost of the design is determined in this stage. The best design is chosen on the basis of how much it meets the goal?

In the **D**esign phase, a high level and detailed design are selected for the substitute. The elements of different designs are put together to build a higher-level design. Once the designing is done, a prototype is made to better understand the possible errors and where to make improvements.

In the **V**erify phase, a team confirms that the design made is approved by all stakeholders. The operability of the design is tested in the real world if it will be a success? Several production and pilot runs will be made to make sure that the quality is at its finest. The design is checked if it is up to expectations, distribution is expanded and all the lessons are well documented. The verify step also has a backup plan to change the product or service to a repetitive operation and make sure that it can be modified.

Getting started with any project requires careful study about the possible outcomes and errors, which is required to be done within the production process. The organizations looking to work with Six Sigma methodology focuses on identifying an issue and how to tackle it with day to day operations.

It is possible to compare DMAID and DMADV with each other and how their phases differ from one and other. The basic concept of both methodologies, however, stays the same to make use of such a process that eliminates waste and gives a near-perfect product.

Tools used in DMADV

DMADV stands for Define, Measure, Analyze, Design and Verify. The DMADV comes under the methodology of implementing Six Sigma. Knowing what tools can be used in the five phases of DMADV makes it easy to implement the methodology.

Define

Define phase describes the goals of design activity.

The following tools can be used in the Define phase:

- Analytical Hierarchy
- QFD

Measure

Measure Phase describes the crucial to shareholders quantitative assessment

The tool used in the Measure phase is:

- SMART (Specific, Measurable, Achievable, Relevant, and Time-based) to translate the needs of customers into the goals of the project.

Analyze

Analyze Phase describes the available options to meet the objectives.

The following tools can be used in the Analyze phase:

- Hypothesis Testing
- Correlation
- Regression

Design

The design phase is used to make new services, products or processes.

The tools used in the design phase are:

- Predictive Models
- Prototypes
- Simulation
- Pilot runs

Verify

Verify phase is to check the working of the product in the real world.

The tools used in the Verify Phase are:

- Control Charts
- Poka-Yoke
- Flagging

Value Stream Mapping

Value stream Mapping comes under the lean-management method for understanding the present situation and making future procedures from the initial stage to the final stage of the product or service, having minimum wastage as much as possible as compared to current mapping. Value stream mapping focuses on the parts of an organization that adds value to a service or a product. The value chain is the complete process within a firm.

A value chain is a set of certain actions that a company in a specific industry performs to deliver a valuable product or service. Value stream mapping can further be said as a firm procedure to understand, modify and document the flow of information needed to produce a product or service.

Value Stream Mapping is generally different in four ways from the Six Sigma's process mapping:

1. It uses and displays a greater range of information than an average process map.
2. It is at a higher level than a lot of process maps.
3. It is at a higher level from raw material to delivering finished goods.
4. It is much focus on getting to know where to focus on projects in future, kaizen events and subprojects.

The value stream map not only defines the product's activity but also takes into account the information systems and management that upkeep the basic procedure. The process is extremely helpful when it comes to reducing the processing time, as the business knows how to make the right decision before the process.

Value stream mapping purpose

The value stream mapping helps in removing the waste in value streams and increasing efficiency. Waste removal is tackled to increase productivity and making leaner operation which in return makes it easy to identify quality problems and waste.

Types of Waste

In 1995, Daniel T. Jones identified seven types of generally accepted wastes. The terms are updated from the original terminology of the Toyota Production System.

Faster than necessary pace: The abundant production of a good or services that results in damage to quality, production flow, and productivity. Known previously as overproduction leading to time and storage wastage.

Waiting: The time when goods are sitting idle and not being worked on or transported.

Conveyance: The procedure when goods are moved around. Known previously as transport, and includes excessive movement and double handling.

Processing: A highly difficult solution for a simple process. Known previously as inappropriate processing, and has unsafe production. It generally leads to poor arrangement and communication and unneeded movement.

Excess Stock: The over-purchasing of an inventory giving rise to higher lead times, increasing the difficulty to identify problems, and substantial storage costs. Previously known as pointless inventory.

Unnecessary Motion: Ergonomic waste which consumes the energy of employees through bending, stretching and picking up objects. Known previously as unnecessary movements and generally avoidable.

Correction of mistakes: Any cost incurred on defects or the resources needed to correct them.

Waste Removal operations

In 1994, Monden identified three types of operations:

- **Non-Value adding operations:** Actions that must be eliminated from the process like waiting.
- **Necessary but non-value adding:** Actions that create waste but run with the current operating procedures.
- **Value-Adding:** The processing or conversion of raw materials through manual labor.

A deeper look at Value Stream Mapping

Value stream mapping has all the aspects of production required to make a product including non-value added and value-added products.

How does Value Steam Mapping works?

The value stream mapping includes:

Illustrating flows of information and materials in a process graphically. It demonstrates the collaboration between the various organizational steps including manufacturing and subsidiary functions.

Marking the problematic sectors, defects, inefficiencies, bottlenecks in an efficient manner as it incorporates and draws material flows, information flows according to their sequence. It even displays the time between two steps and the cycle time.

Involving all shareholders of the company at every step of the process making it easier to change the company's culture and face the countermeasures arising due to it. It gives a defined presentation of all the factors that limits a company from reaching its full potential.

Aids the kaizen methodology as the direction can be devoted towards lean transformation teams, upper management, and front line supervisors.

How to build and use a Value Stream Map?

Step 1: Know where you stand

Understanding the current position of your business is important. Choose the product or line of products and decide where it can be improved then train the group working on it for value stream mapping. A cross-functional group should be picked and have all the shareholders involved within the process. Once the group has been selected, know the material flow's physical path.

It is important that all the primary and secondary material flows of the manufacturing process are mapped. While understanding all the material flow paths, watch and make notes of all the communication points with care. This will help to work out the value stream map's current state.

Look for the starting and finishing points of your process.

At the end of your process, the owner is the final person playing the role on when a course will initiate and end. In value stream analysis, this is quite different the initiation of a process begins when a request is made by a customer the point they get the product. Arguments could raise about taking the process by adding things like transaction settlement.

Sketch the process flow

Include sub-steps in your map, this will help to give a clear picture of one unit flowing through the process. Mark the areas that need inputs or outputs. Does these changes change your map? Is there a missing step? Get all this clear by including external groups with the map.

Measure each step of the process

What measures you take depend on what kind of project you are doing. What you can afford to measure?

The measurements depend on the project you are doing. What is your potential to measure? Some processes are expensive and complex to measure.

Before stepping in to measure make sure that your measuring procedure is up to date and are accurate with a reproducibility and repeatability study. Measurements can consume a lot of your time, so getting it done right the very first time is important.

Know the boundaries of your process. What will suit your business best and what will be the worst and ask yourself these questions:

- What is the normal time?
- What is moderate time?
- Is there any time spent on preparation?
- What are the resources use for certain step?
- What is the idle time?
- How many man are put to use?
- How many work shifts are required?

- How much the machine can produce efficiently?
- How much of the work can be completed and delivered
- What will be the inventory size after this process?

Step 2: Calculate and Respond

Calculate the current position of the value stream map with all the shareholder of the company to get data on process's current performance. Understand the defects, deficiencies, bottlenecks, and limiting factors of the current process.

The efficiency and cost of each restraining factors should be taken in numbers. Dig out the root cause of the limiting factor, and develop effective solutions for it rather than looking at the symptoms of the limitations. Modify the value stream map for corrections that displays the solutions and eliminates the process's limiting factors. The value stream map now is called the future state value stream map.

Understand the value being given as an output and how much waste is incurred. The wastes can be rework time, retooling, downtime, idle time, etc.

Make note for process steps that don't add value or are unnecessary to production. Understand that:

- How to know if a step isn't valuable or valuable?

Remind yourself about the value-added activities

- Is the process done right the first time?
- Are customers willing to purchase it?
- Is there a physical change in the object's process?

Know the cycle time

Cycle time is the time a completed service or physical product takes to finish all steps of production to complete one product or service. The total time taken to complete a process is different than the overall time taken to complete a step. The cycle time can be best understood by an example, it is the time when a customer orders a product from your company and it is the time taken to produce and deliver the product to the customer.

Step 3: Modify

Know how to make changes to the process:

- How can the identified wastes be cut out, removed, avoided from the process?
- What are the steps that slow down production or cycle time?
- Can the process be made more efficient?
- What the bottlenecks of the process?

Before using the future state value stream map, get in touch with the shareholders of the company and present the steps needing improvement. Once the points are approved provide training to the team according to new requirements and process. Now implement the changes in a descending priority basis to ease the process.

The aim shouldn't be to perfect a single step but rather to give the customer highest level of satisfaction with efficiency. Efficiency means to deliver the best products with least use of resources and with minimum wastage.

Step 4: Maintain

Once the future state value stream map has been adopted by the company, make sure to monitor and reinforce the new procedure on a continuous basis. The process adopted should be cross-checked with cost-related, performance measuring, and establishment parameters to know the impacts on the production process.

Value stream mapping can be a great way to brainstorm and understand what a customer needs and what is being actually provided by the company. Value stream mapping is a calculated plan of a set of actions which is put by a team to add value to any company's process resulting in better efficiency overall.

What is Process Mining?

Process Mining is an investigative technique that intends to find, screen and improve genuine processes by separating knowledge effectively from accessible occasion logs in the frameworks of current data. Process mining looks for a showdown between event information and process models with graphical analysis to support the diagnosis. It makes it easy to check consistency, identifying deviations, foresee delays, bolster basic leadership and suggestions for process upgrades.

Process Mining is a group of systems in the field of process management that helps the analysis of business processes with the logs. It plans to improve process productivity and comprehension. it's also called Automated Business Process Discovery (ABPD). Also, in scholastic literature the term "ABPD" is utilized in a more restricted way; it is considered as the methods that input event logs and produce business process models. But process mining is a wider term overall and it is not just restricted to it.

In the process mining, special data mining algorithms are used to tell about patterns, trends, and other information present in the event log.

Steps of Process Mining

Process mining comprises of two primary steps:

Step 1: Choosing the process and its prioritization, which obviously sets up the improvement goals and distinguishes where the business value is made in various places of the company also how high-level processes influence the formation of significant worth.

Step 2: Gaining the process data that needs improvement that can change it into a process model.

Application of Process Mining

The utilization of Process Mining in an association offers the following capabilities:

- Improvement of existing or past process models through extra information from spared records

- Understanding of alternate point of views on activities rather than just on process viewpoint

- Situation testing, prescription examination, predictive analysis through relevant information

- Automated revelation and examination of client associations, just as an arrangement with internal processes

- Monitoring of key execution performances through dashboard continuously.

- Data planning and purifying support

- Group of various process models that communicate with one another in a solitary mining panel

- Effective participation among Business and IT

- Making business process standardized

- Improving processes for advanced operational excellence

- Self-operating discovery of process models, special cases and instances of processes with insights and fundamental frequencies

Three Classes of Process Mining Techniques

The three classes of process mining techniques are as follows:

1. Discovery: With the help of process mining algorithms, it takes an event log and creates a process model without utilizing any earlier data.

2. Conformance: Analyze the deviations or wasteful aspects between the process model of business and perfect processes. The event log process and the relating process models are compared, and the differences are noted.

3. Enhancement: With data of genuine process, process models are adjusted and improved.

Process Mining for Different Sectors
Process Mining works perfectly fine for different sectors:

Manufacturing

Fast and exact delivery to a client is a definitive object in any manufacturing business. If a business/company resides in more than one region, there could be a difference in the quality of delivered goods in different parts of the region because of process steps included, duration, cost and workers performing several tasks, etc. All event data could be available in a system dashboard for use in Process Mining. Making an effective policy and cut out the differences in minor or major productions of items can ensure keeping the same quality with accurate delivery to a customer every time.

Banking and Financial

In the financial regions, it is a must to adhere to the principles and guidelines – the proof is also required to be fair with the regulation. You can picture even individual cases as a process stream by utilizing the event data from the framework. Frequent deviations and varieties can be seen with process mining, and also the explanation causing non-conformance. Process mining can not only show actions but also leads to improvements that can be induced.

Retail

The achievement of retail organizations originates from proficient business tasks. Co-ordination, estimation, management of warehouses, orders and suppliers, all things make the retailing organization to work. Process Mining offers an in-sight for connected processes giving comprehension of bottlenecks and any other hurdle that might hinder the processing. Process mining also gives the data-based findings that help to focus on the advancement of those regions that are most important and give the most noteworthy business results.

Telecommunication

Capacity to improve operational processes is vital to progress and gain results especially in telecommunication as it is an exceptionally focused sector all around the world. Process Mining supports media transmissions to broad visibility to geographically scatter operations, also to point out bottlenecks. It guarantees the delivery of services and products to the customers on schedule.

Management Consulting

Counseling organizations have a significant job in the improvement of many industries. No matter the size, counseling organizations use Process Mining to accomplish data-driven improvement which depends on certainties rather than presumptions.

Utilities

Utility organizations hold popularity for strong and dependable administrations for their clients. Process Mining gives insights into the complete far and wide procedures recognizing key reasons and bottlenecks.

Services

Process mining is a significant apparatus for improving the proficiency of a service company. By guaranteeing coordinated tasks, discovering key reasons for the issues and ineffectiveness of the company, process mining leads towards betterment. Since the business logic of service organizations is to accomplish higher operation goals in terms of lower costs than their competitors.

Why Select Process Mining?

You cannot trust what your heart and mind say, neither can you trust a hunch. You need definite fact-based figures to work with. You should have the option to respond rapidly and not go with surveys that are already outdated. You need truth-based figures to back up your cases. Using updated technology leads the organization to achieve its desired goals. When you need to work with data, it is better to go with process mining as it is applicable to almost all the sectors. You can go for it because it:

- **Saves time in data collection:**

Overseeing and advancing processes is one of the most concentrated zones that requires a great deal of time for BPM (Business Process Management) professionals. When their data analysis phase is completed, the information on which they are backing their suppositions just changes over time. Working so long for what? Futile! happens so often. So how might we conquer this issue?

Process Mining gives you a head start by robotizing the most tedious part i.e. gathering information. Data collection is no doubt the most time-consuming part. What is happening and being executed must be understood in order to understand the idea of basic operation situation in any organization, and not what seems to occur. This is what you get from process mining.

- **Locates process bottlenecks**

Processing bottlenecks are often so difficult to reveal by facilitating BPM or process mapping workshops. Individuals have a hunch/premonition of what could not be right or wasteful, however, they need the information to back their suppositions. Process Mining works like a charm when it is about processing information using actual fact-based figures. It doesn't make an assumption but actually talks about facts and figures. By finding the right problems at the right time, it can save time as well as resources.

Bring facts not opinions

With process mining, you don't need to agree with mid-points to uncover the explanations for irresponsible behavior. The option to see a 10,000-foot view of an organization's business process and still have the option to penetrate down the bottlenecks and key cause of deviations is one of the basic fundamental objectives of process mining. It can detect the root cause of the problem without any trouble.

Lean Six Sigma and Process Mining

Like process mining, the processing of Lean Six Sigma doesn't depend on the hypothesis. It is a data-driven approach that needs to be back up with special key figures. Automation of the process is one way to improve it, thus process mining offers the best solution to implement Lean Six Sigma.

Lean Six Sigma needs proper data to work with, and process mining provides it as it works as a data tracer. As we have previously mentioned in this chapter that Lean Sigma uses the DMAIC cycle, process mining can be used in its every aspect.

1. **Define:** In this initial step, a project is defined with its essential targets and customer demands. It also defines the present status of the process. Here the process mining can provide the visual of the process flow in real.

2. **Measure:** For measurement, proper data is needed and that's what process mining does. You can use the numbers to get the output which then can be traced to track the issues and troubles. With process mining, data collection is possible for one process and many at a single time.

3. **Analyze**: During this step, issues are acknowledged with their causes. With process mining, it becomes easy to find out where the problem occurs in the first place and why it leads to the disturbance. Within a few minutes, you are able to detect the issue based on the real facts and figures and design the action.

4. **Improve:** By reaching this step, your process has become free from the waste, which is the major goal to go for Lean Six Sigma in the first place. The product must jump from one step to another without producing any waste at all after the solution has been integrated. Now using process mining here provides the information if anything other than the desired process might come into the process. When the actual plan is

different from the one that is happening, you can easily detect the issue.

5. **Control:** Finding the issue and solving it doesn't cease the Lean Six Sigma work. The new improved process must now be monitored deeply. The process mining in this step can inform about the achieved improvements in real-time. It allows you to keep a check on the processes even when the Lean Six Sigma project is ended and detects the changes for immediate changes when necessary.

Lean Six Sigma and process mining complement each other and they are applied in diverse sectors together. When work side by side, they save time, reduce cost, improves sales, enhance customer satisfaction, and even allow the follow-up on the completed projects.

Chapter V: Adopting and Modifying Six Sigma for Use

Improvements of Six Sigma

Lean Six Sigma leads towards the improvement of the overall process; it helps the organization to achieve its goals in the best possible way. For the improved implementation of Lean Six Sigma, it is better to identify the next best Lean Six Sigma project beforehand.

It might be easy to identify which techniques to use, but it is hard to select the correct project. Different experts have their opinion on how to identify the improvement project but methods of some stand out from others.

Why Choose Improvement Projects?

Choosing the correct project is essential for gaining the desired results. One right project can have a remarkable impact on the outcomes of an organization. When everything turns out fine, the results may appear within a period of six months.

Choosing the correct project not only leads to the satisfaction of the customers but employees as well because they will feel connected to making improvements overall.

When the project is selected without giving proper consideration, the results might not be near to ideal and will lead to the waste of energy, time, money, and resources. The improper selection might also lead to an obstacle that will affect the process of the organization for many days after its removal.

Other than the assets, the team might also suffer and lose faith in the changes that you are willing to implement with Lean Six Sigma. The project managers may find it hard to make the team again when a new project is pointed out for improvement. Even for the current project, the management might lose attention.

Thus, it is recommended by the experts to give proper time and consideration while selecting the project. The right project yields positive results and makes everyone happy by reserving time, money, and resources.

Which Project to Select First?

In one organization, there can be many projects that require attention and improvement. When there is more than one project, the management needs to decide where it is necessary to make the improvement. It is impossible to consider every problem at once, thus the selection becomes vital.

When identifying the improvement project, one can use the following means:

Identifying the project with the help of the management

Determine the three biggest issues that your business faces by taking the help of the management. The selected project must directly address any one or more of the issues. The team must remove any hurdle that comes in a way of solving the issue. The management team should extract the information by using different mediums within the organization.

The benefit of using this method to identify the problem is that employees know their involvement which improves their performance when the results come out better than before. The team must ask everyone involved if they see any issue.

Although this method involves everyone within the organization and employees feel heard, it may have some drawbacks. Project identification with this method cannot detect the actual size of the problem that is needed to be handled. Also, there's a probability that only a handful of contributors consider it a problem, and the actual issue is way too bigger than that.

To solve the issue associated with this selection of the improvement project, only experienced people should be involved in extracting the real issue. They must use an efficient approach. By using correct statistics, it becomes easy to highlight where improvement is required in an area. All the issues should be considered one after another but making the timeline is a must.

Identifying the project with the help of the customers

Customer's satisfaction is the ultimate goal of implementing Six Sigma in the company's processes. Take the help of the customer service team to extract the three biggest issues that your customers are facing. Utilize every forum where your customers had launched any complaint. You can also initiate a short survey to see what issues your customers are facing in your services or products. Statically arrange your collected data to see which complaints are on the top. This will help in choosing the right project that will fulfill the demands of the customers.

There is no major drawback of this method as your customers are the ones who are getting your products and services. They are the consumers so they can tell better. But many times, it becomes difficult to identify the real issue. The customers are diverting away from you because someone else is providing better products or services within their range. So, it might become tricky to get to the actual problem when the customers are not straight forward in telling the issue.

Identifying the project using operation performance indicators

The most structured form of selecting the improvement project is through operation performance indicators. It analyzes factors like mistakes, lead times, incidents, claims, etc. Identifying the project where the indicator markers present bad results helps in aligning the data to see which process must be corrected first according to the Lean Six Sigma approach.

One problem with using this factor solely is that it doesn't involve employees and their ideas. Also, the measuring tool might not be efficient enough to provide the correct data.

All in all, one method might not be satisfactory to identify the major problems in the process. To identify improvement projects, one or all the methods can be used to select the correct project. The project selection is the first thing in the Lean Six Sigma implementation and it must be done with great care. When the start is good, only then the desired results could be achieved. But when there is a flaw in the project selection, many problems could arise that can diminish the company goals greatly.

What To Do After Identifying the Improvement Project?

Selecting the improvement project is one thing but then implementing the Lean Six Sigma technique is the main goal. Not every selected project is manageable. It must be realistic to achieve the desired goals.

You need to analyze the project timeline. It should be completed within a particular period and the team must know the deadline. When the project is unable to achieve the presumed goals within the given timeframe, it might create frustration in the team.

Alongside this, the capacity of the process must also be clearly defined. You must measure your project and see where improvements are needed. Without measuring, it is impossible to define where to head.

Once the project is defined now you must know how to proceed with the project. Among all the methods available for Lean Six Sigma implementation, here are the four steps that are highly convenient to use. To identify the improvement project, you can use them step by step:

Step 1: A Lucid Strategic Plan

As you know the first task is to determine the project on which Lean Six Sigma could be applied. It is also necessary to be acquainted with your organization's key plan when making this selection.

One strategic planning process may have the following components:

- Planning to design: Create a guide to achieve the strategic plan; you need to do it before using the above mentioned technique
- Examine Values: Check the interests of the Lean Six Sigma contributors
- Mission Plan: Create a mission statement by using the recommendations and bits of advice of the stakeholders
- Business Demonstration: Create a suitable plan of action, keeping in mind these things including social contemplations, organization culture, and available finances for either rebuilding the existing business lines or the expansion of new business lines
- Performance Review: Do the audit of the organization for the financial basis as well as for the abilities to execute the task on hand

- Examine Gap: Compare the present execution with the ideal state to measure any lacking if present
- Integrating Activity Plans: Actualize and create a definite arrangement to achieve the methodologies of the organization to end the gap if any
- Detour When Required: Develop alternative courses of action to counter potential market fluctuations; stay focus and weigh different situations that may influence the strategic plan and organization's capacity to conduct the process according to the plan
- Implementation: Implement the changes within the organization by means of tumbled goals, recognizing proprietors, time periods, and quantifiable execution measures.

Initially, organizations should strategically close apparent holes that may hinder the activity arrangement later. Commonly, strategic thrusts are activities with clear sanctions and spending plans; they have no loopholes. Senior officials create these strategy having clear responsibilities of everyone involved.

Strategic thrusts may be explicit or reserved, contingent upon the apparent holes. Strategic thrusts include Six Sigma, Lean Six Sigma, Six Sigma designs, and everything in it.

Step 2: Logically Improve Strategy

The subsequent advancement is to see how enhancement exercises ought to be lined up with the action plans initiated in the strategic plan.

An analysis will most likely distinguish where 'Line of business' or 'LOB' appears according to the current competition and market growth as a part of the business displayed in the strategic plan step.

The plan is to decide a powerful methodology for a specific line of business depending on the pace of market development and the company's competition for LOB.

For instance, a specific line of business holds a solid competition in a quickly growing market, the supervisory group for the lines of business may push product advancement over other operations of the organization to meet the market demand. Then again, a specific LOB with a frail competition in a moderate market may require a broad center around improvement of process cost utilizing Lean Six Sigma.

For different situations, the improvement process must be fit into the optimization of every particular line of business comparative with its key objectives. This is the duty of the management to decide which thing comes first.

Step 3: Execution of the Policy Deployment System

After setting the strategy, it is time to add the action plans into the organization's policy.

Leaders must realize that it is important to function according to the policy deployment system. They will have to give up many of their past actions in favor of new ones that would boost an organization's objectives. Also, an organization should comprehend that employees need gears and drills to perform new duties excellently and professionally.

Effective execution of policy deployment includes:

- Setting elevated objectives, targets, time periods and proprietors depending on the action within the strategic plan

- Setting practical and departmental objectives, targets, allotment of time, and proprietors reliant on maintaining the substantial level objectives to the local level

- Integration of close objectives into implementation plans for teams or sole individuals

- Performing ordinary execution reviews for significant level and local objective accomplishments

- Integration of executing objectives in the reward structure for the executives

Step 4: Knowing Basic Business Processes

Every Organization works under some structure as a framework that changes their inputs into output. Their input includes the working, information, raw material, or anything of the customer's use that turns into the desired output that is their service or product. The whole process works under a definite system to gain the organization's goals and customer's desires. Organizations apparently keep records of their processes.

To explain what to look at in the execution process for opening doors towards development, the accompanying terms apply:

- L1 process: L1 is also called Level One; it is a central business process that is compatible with the working of the organization. It also features bookkeeping and other process tracing mechanisms.

- L2 process: Renowned as Level Two process, it is the subprocess of Level One. It includes unambiguously related order of planned steps.

- Work steps: A coherent work unit of a Level two process that includes an order of work tasks usually done by a sole individual or a little group.

The regular way to deal with distinguishing open doors for development is to initially comprehend what key L1 processes are inside the organization. At that point, the key L1 process will be separated so the L2 process can be distinguished. A normal Lean Six Sigma venture at that point will define an arrangement of work ventures inside at least one or more level two processes.

Lean Six Sigma has the potential to improve, but for that, the right approach is needed from the beginning to the end.

Deployment Mistakes of Six Sigma

Making mistakes in deploying Six Sigma procedures leads to unwanted results. Not only it costs time but it also wastes valuable resources. Implementation of Six Sigma could only be successful with designing a well-managed process plan with efficient resource and time administration. Whether a Six Sigma practitioner is new or a pro, there's always a chance of a mistake in a complex project. The successful Six Sigma implementation results in the benefit of all the people involved; it is even fruitful for the consumers. On the other hand, when there are flaws in the process, there are many drawbacks overall.

Most Common Mistakes and Their Solutions

There are some most common mistakes that organizations usually overlook when implementing the Six Sigma process.

Step 1: Unsuitable Strategy:

The execution technique is useful for coordinating the targets of the organization. Although the end result is never the one you expected all the time, strategy development is a time-intensive and messy process. Often in this process, organizations fail to distinguish between what they exist to do and what they must do in order to survive, that confusion leads to rudderless strategy making.

When the strategy is faulty to initiate the project with, how it can improve the process overall?

Solution

To accomplish the desired outcomes, implementation of the Six Sigma process must be in accordance with the objectives of an organization. It should include the organization's calendar with an emphasis on what could be done. It is necessary to monitor the progress and the changes associated with it that have altered the results. After the evaluation, one can see what is important and make the modification accordingly. Noticeable changes in the results of the organization will give employees more trust in Six Sigma that will lead to more energetic work.

When making the strategy, it is necessary to understand the current situation of the organization. It is something that should be customized according to the company rather than copying what others are doing. One strategy that is beneficial for one organization might not produce the same results for others. Basics of Six Sigma deployment will remain the same but it may need some changes depending on a company that should be considered from the very beginning by the experts.

Step 2: Wrong leadership

Awful administration prompts poor representative maintenance and demotivates the rest of the workers. Devotion from the executives is among the fundamentals for the progress of the organization. Administrators must show how Six Sigma functions and should always emphasize it at all levels. Not only just the mangers of Six Sigma should back up the significance of this practice but also the team member from different departments should take the part.

Solution

A terrible initiative can genuinely affect employees' morale and even cause the company's bottom line to plunge. Since supporting Six Sigma is significant, additional consideration should be paid to all members from the leaders of the organization to workers. Management must convey its significance to all and elaborate on how it coordinates with the goals of the entire organization. Effectively taken feedbacks from the involved employees should be considered for making changes to meet the goals. Also, constructive feedback on the progress of the employees creates a positive working environment that produces better results.

The leader must connect with the employees. The workers usually don't commit to an organization; instead, they commit with their leader. Sharing the strategy and the future motives of the organization make them more aware of what is happening which inturn produces beneficial outcomes. A right leader will not only implement the Six Sigma goal successfully but also set an example that is to be followed by all.

Step 3: Unnecessary focus on training and certification

Six Sigma certifications and training is vital for employees because they ensure an optimal level of qualification that allows performing a certain task. This induces a specific competition in an organization. The team becomes highly focused on getting certification and training only. Without intention, many times workers get too centered with the competition that they carry away from the basic goal to execute projects. The unhealthy competition also creates problems and produces a tougher working environment for all.

Solution

Loose belts can be tightened again with proper coaching and instruction. Teams ought to consistently accomplish the objectives of an organization and should concentrate on choosing the correct Six Sigma ventures. The management should run routine checks to make alterations when an absence of progress is noted.

There is no denial in the significance of the Six Sigma certification and training, but the correct implementation should be the focus. When the focus is on academics only, the organization will fail to produce the desired results. Also, one training after another won't be fruitful unless the outcome of one training has been evaluated before moving on to the other.

Competition is a good thing, but it should not be only for increasing the numbers of certificates. Quality comes before quantity. Teams should be rewarded upon their productivity and not on their knowledge only.

Step 4: Poor Project Selection

Overall, the planning of a project is the most important stage in project management. Inadequate focus on choosing the right project can lead to projects that lack sufficient data to begin with. It might not even be suitable for the organization itself. Likewise, deep concentration might set past the capabilities of Green and Black belts resulting in postponing and rejection of projects. It might also lead to confusion among different levels of employees. Here, too much focus as well as too little focus, both can lead to a problem.

Solution

Objectives can not generally be accomplished unless teams are sure that the selected Six Sigma undertakings depend on calculated information. While choosing the project, attention should be given to the objectives of an organization, its working, customers, and finances. When these things are not considered, no matter what the Six Sigma project plans say, the results are unachievable.

The selection of series also matters here. Which project to initiate first and which should come next should also be considered.

Step 5: Lack of responsibility

Workers are primarily focused on their own advancement and progress inside the organization, but every employee is equally responsible for the effective implementation of any plan. Also, it is not always necessary that every member of the team is working ideally. They may dodge their responsibilities, blame others for mistakes, try to avoid difficult tasks, and depend on others' work and bits of advice. This could be because of a lack of trust in a team or a manager.

There might also be the issue of the communication –
the management might not be able to fully converse the
benefits of implementation of Six Sigma to the most
vital contributor. This all results in lowering the
implementation impression and the team might resist
the new process.

Solution

Problems can arrive when employees here and there
don't take responsibility for their actions. Teams should
join the objectives of the organization under the Six
Sigma implementation. The goals of Six Sigma,
organization motive, and personal goals, all are
interconnected. To convey this message to all, the team
can pick up some help from any of the workers in the
organization.

The vital part is to communicate the implementation of
Six Sigma. The leaders will have to consistently
highlight the importance of usage of Six Sigma and how
its outcomes will benefit the whole team. Not only just
workers and teams, leaders and upper management
should also follow up with the Six Sigma
implementation to target goals.

Step 6: Blinding trusting measurement system

The measuring tools form the basis of the Six Sigma
foundation. Data and measurements are very important
while deploying Six Sigma in any process. Many times,
even the pros are unable to find the mistake and the
end results are unachievable because they trust the
measuring system blindly.

Solution

Measurement system analysis is very important for carrying out Six Sigma efficiently. Checking the measuring tools before initiating any task must be an important step to follow.

Step 7: Fail to incorporate technology

Technology advancement has improved many processes. It makes working better and produces faster results. One cannot leave behind the software and technology and do great with Six Sigma – they must be used together. Many times, leadership or workers fail to incorporate technology because of a lack of knowing how it works, or how it must be used.

Solution

The right stakeholder who is technology advanced should be approached. Using technology and updated software programs are helpful in achieving the desired goal earlier. They also make things easy to manage. If the team is not tech-savvy, they should be trained separately to manage things using the modern technology. A correct approach to a process is necessary rather than just hurrying up to implement the change.

These all are the mistakes that are common in any organization implementing Six Sigma techniques for the first time. But with time, and using the right techniques, the outcomes could be improved many folds.

Other than the above-mentioned major mistakes, organizations might do any of the following mistakes that fail Six Sigma procedure for them; they are:

Lack of appropriate resources: Six Sigma could not be effective when any of its key ingredients is missing. Probably, the project has everything but the timeline is not sufficient, there is not enough supply of good, or a team may lack a vital player.

Lack of Potential Business Impact knowledge: Potential Business Impact should be among the initial things that must be calculated under DMAIC because when there is no knowledge of it, the project might get affected greatly.

Lack of Key Stakeholders' Support: The key skateholders must provide the support for the project. When there is no support for them, the project could not run successfully.

Lack of Scope: When there is lack of scope, the project could not achieve its desired results. The project charter must contain all the aims of the project and how it should be executed.

What is Poka-Yoke?

Poka-Yoke is a common term that is present side by side to Six Sigma mistakes.

Mistake-proofing in Japan is called as Poka-Yoke. In literal Japanese terms, it can be translated as 'resistance to errors'. This method was introduced by Shigeo Shingo in 1961 when working with Toyota Motor Corporation.

 It can be defined as the action needed to remove or lower the chance of error or the ability to make an error in Six Sigma. It is not a difficult tool to understand; it is merely simple in nature. Its philosophy is very similar to that of Six Sigma and can be used to achieve the goals of Six Sigma.

Poka-Yoke has great diversity when it comes to its application; it can be applied in the processes of engineering, manufacturing, and transactional activities. It revolves around developing the actions that can help in removing defects and errors in day-to-day processes.

There is nothing fancy about these actions. It could be a mere physical action like making a checklist, highlighting something on a form, or just shifting the series of operations. But once the defect is pointed out by the Poka-Yoke, it demands immediate action with correction.

Lean Six Sigma and Poka-Yoke

According to Poka-Yoke, there are different reasons for error but they could be avoided if the people are able to see the problem from the start while forming the steps to follow. It defines the reasons and shows where to make necessary changes. Removing the defect in the process before it appears is the correct approach of defect reduction, that lowers process cost as well as save many resources. The same ideology should be followed when using Lean Six Sigma in any process.

Everyone contributing to Lean Six Sigma implementation in the processes of the organization must see the flaw from the start. The process should only be initiated once the major problems are solved.

Chapter VI: Six Sigma Certification and Criticism

What is the Six Sigma Certification?

Learning Six Sigma methodologies can do wonders for your life and help put a huge impact on the future of your career. The addition of Six Sigma Certification on your resume puts a sign of commitment that will help improve your business expertise and analytical skills. The addition will overall improve the business where you working.

The Six Sigma implementations can be found across the globe in numerous organizations like Credit Suisse, Boeing, United States Army, Amazon, General Electric, Bank of America, Starwood Hotels, and Ford Motor Company.

A Short Background

In 1986, Bill Smith developed Six Sigma, an engineer at Motorola Company aimed to improve the devices of the company which wasn't according to the quality standards. His approach was based on quality control and statistical methods shown by Ronald Fisher, Edwards Deming, and Walter Shewhart.

- Sir Ronald Aylmer Fisher is the single most important person in 20th-century statistics. His known work is popular in today's world like Student's P-Value, F-distribution, t-distribution, and others.

- Edwards Deming worked in Japan and played an important role in shaping quality control in Japanese production processes. He is recognized with developing the sampling techniques used by the Bureau of Labor Statistics and Department of Census in the US.

- Walter Shewhart developed SQC (Statistical Quality Control) and also pioneer PDCA (Plan Do Check Act) model also called the Shewhart Cycle.

Six Sigma is a set of methodologies used by organizations to make improvements to their production processes, guarantee quality and eliminate defects. Getting Six Sigma certification helps in authorizing the professional capable of identifying errors, defects, or risks in the business process and help to remove them.

Six Sigma Certification commonly includes professionals to have some level of experience and prove their efficiency. The certificate helps an individual to become an expert in improving processes and enhance his/her authority.

Six Sigma Certification Levels

The Six Sigma is divided into different levels:

- White Belt
- Yellow Belt
- Green Belt
- Black Belt
- Master Black Belt

These certifications are obtainable by getting accreditation from a body like ASQ (American Society for Quality).

Six Sigma White Belt

The most basic or entry-level certification deals with basics of Six Sigma concepts. White belts are helpful for an organization's change management and involve with company's problem-solving teams who help with projects.

Six Sigma Yellow Belt

This level provides Six Sigma's specifics, how and where they are applicable. You will be able to help project teams with problem-solving.

Six Sigma Green Belt

This level of advanced analysis is understood and helps in resolving problems regarding quality. Green belts lead the projects and help black belts in gathering data and analyzing.

Six Sigma Black Belt

Black belts are the professionals and experts of change. They provide training along with leading the projects.

Six Sigma Master Black Belt

The highest level of Six Sigma achievement is the Master Black Belt. This level professionals design strategies, develop key performance indicators, coach green, and black belts, and act as a consultant.

Is Six Sigma really that important? The idea of this can be best understood from case studies of different who adopted Six Sigma which is given below. Six Sigma process helped General Electric to put $350 million in savings back in 1998. Motorola allocated its highest savings by 2005, of $17 billion. After a decade GE was able to increase that amount over $1 billion.

Six Sigma Certification Benefits for Individuals

The Six Sigma certification isn't just another addition to your resume the certification comes with a lot of advantages for companies and individuals.

Improve business processes and durable quantity improvement

Once done with Six Sigma certification you will be investigating the manufacturing and business processes of a company and take actions to improve them. You will be able to do a complete evaluation of company's current procedures and assess how they affect the quality.

The certification displays that you are able to reach the durable quality that the firm is looking forward to.

Keeping check of processes carefully to make sure that there isn't any deviation from the meanwhile taking right actions to bring projects back online which were deviating from path.

Having value in every industry

Being a highly demanded methodology in industries. Six Sigma techniques are useful in electronics, aerospace, telecom, financial services, IT, marketing, banking, HR and various industries.

Industries certified in Six Sigma have knowledge in many different methods which can be opted to streamline business processes, reduce costs, improve employee acceptance, and increase revenue, all these lead to an improved bottom line in any industry.

The Six Sigma certification earns an individual the title of a change agent in any organization. Working alongside teams further refines the leadership skills and adding more value to the individual.

Ensure Compliance

Six Sigma requires extremely high-quality standards. This is the reason a noteworthy number of procurers, vendors and oversight organizations use Six Sigma Standards when reviewing products. Individuals with Six Sigma certification can help their company with profitable contracts and working with international standards.

Rise to higher positions

Once done with Six Sigma certification an individual gets a clear picture of how to make maximum profit from any Six Sigma project. The certification helps individuals in getting financial management and risk assessment skills. These types of skills are always in demand for top-level and middle-level managerial positions.

Greater Salary

Six Sigma Certification is not easy to get, there are lot of studies, and the exams are tough. Furthermore, getting from one belt level to another requires years of actual work. For this reason, Six Sigma Certified individuals are the highest paid professionals in the world having pay bracket above $100,000.

Get practical experience in Quality Management

The Six Sigma training program provides individuals with practical experience on industrial projects and making use of theories in real-life workplace. Getting started with Six Sigma Certification gets an individual a valued knowledge even before working with a team. The professional acquiring such a certificate is refined to take strategic decisions and tackle the obstacles causing delays in processing.

Six Sigma Certification benefits for Organizations

In 1995, Jack Welch introduced Six Sigma as a key component to General Electric's Business Strategy. From that time, firms have put up Six Sigma to use with major success, the benefits can be seen below:

Higher Productivity

Engineered for the space industry for making new products, Allen medical implemented DMAIC methodology and lean tools for overall improvement to production of Arm boards. The new methodology allowed them to save 45 seconds per arm board production, hence increasing the arm boards produced per hour from 5.3 to a bit over 6.

Lower Costs

Decreasing defects reduced and minimized wastage resulting in overall lower production cost with greater profits. Failing to produce a quality product can get costly. Developing a poor service or product can greatly reduce the cost which is the true meaning of cost of quality.

Raising the client's confidence in one's business

Using Six Sigma can reduce processing steps and increase customer satisfaction. For example, through the use of cross-functional process mapping (CFPM) methodology, Citibank removed the unnecessary steps from their process which resulted in higher customer satisfaction.

Gaining reliability and shareholder's trust

Customers and shareholders trust a company where employees are relatively qualified. A company having a significant number of Six Sigma certified employees it means that quality is expected from that company. A company having quality is competitive in the market and inspires confidence in partners and investors.

Reduce training costs and employee turnover

The DMAIC methodology is applicable to be used in HR management. Research shows that in a multinational company losing millions of dollars because of employee turnover of 35% each year wanted to reduce the numbers to 25%.

After applying Six Sigma methodology, they came to know about few contributing factors which were: low compensation and poor career prospects. The solution was to make use of new hiring processes and training new employees. The outcomes were great reducing the turnover by 10% and saving $1.1 million as a result.

The Six Sigma Progress

The numerous cases of Six Sigma implementation success can be studied from all over the world. It is an internationally accepted standard that can be used in small to high profile organizations. The methodology is a logical and structured approach to develop a chain of continuous improvement.

Six Sigma isn't a destination that stops after accomplishing single milestone instead it is a journey of continuous improvement which doesn't end. The outcomes are excellence and higher customer loyalty with bottom line profits. Implementing Six Sigma is worthwhile for any organization in search of reaching near perfection.

Once the road of implementing Six Sigma has been taken by an organization it doesn't want to get off it. The company sees for itself the benefits of the process as it solves the complexity of the production processes and resolves issues arriving one after the other. The smoothness inflow of the production process is what inspires any company to opt the methodology in very first place.

Criticism of Six Sigma

There are multiple reasons why a business might not be adopting Lean Six Sigma. A few of the reasons can be stated to be valid, a lot can be stated as a misconception, while some stand as pure fictions. The ten common reasons observed over the years are:

Fear of the unknown or failing

The one reason which we can all agree to is the fear of the unknown. The effects of such fear can be paralyzing in the real world and in the business world it can also occur. The fear prevents a business from growing and making it stuck with the same old procedures and outcomes.

Not able to afford Six Sigma

The reason for not adopt the methodology is the fear of finance. It is not a process requiring large capital instead it should be looked as an investment which will give turn your results 5 to 10 times better in a year. A business can get started with Six Sigma after obtaining the Yellow belt certification. However, hiring an external black belt certified professional for training will be a good idea to grow. A business can also buy projects and statistical management software.

Never heard of Lean Six Sigma

This seems to be a valid criticism as Lean Six Sigma is growing in popularity but still, it isn't a part of the normal business language. Many small organizations mainly are unaware that it is present which keeps them behind.

Lean Six Sigma is a trend which will fade away

The presence of Lean Six Sigma can be found since the 19th century with business and quality leaders like Toyota's Shigeo Shingo, Henry Ford, Western Electric's Walter Shewhart, Edwards Deming, Taichi Ohno, and Joseph Juran. Six Sigma has grown over time and is different from other kaizen programs. People think that it might fade away with time, but the improvement techniques are something that an organization always want. The customer's choice is well focused on Lean Six Sigma techniques. So there's little to no chance that it may get lost in time any time sooner.

Lean Six Sigma is too much calculation and statistics

The truth is a lot of companies don't even need advanced mathematics and statistics to get benefitted from Lean Six Sigma. A lot of principles of Six Sigma can easily be applied in any business.

The most powerful amongst all tools is to know the wastes in the process and their types. Planning out a map to point out all the bottlenecks, and gaps in the process. If the employees can understand what the customer needs then arriving at a solution to solve the problem won't be that difficult.

The employees don't necessarily need to be engineers; they can be front line supervisors and trained to work and understand the needs of the customers. Proper training will play its role again and again till the perfection that is expected is reached by the employees.

Don't have time to dedicate to Lean Six Sigma

A company that is not being able to identify the cause of the problem will always be stuck to it. No matter what is done to solve the issue, when the root cause is not defined, the problem will appear again. The only solution to make things right is finding where the problem has been initiating from.

The biggest waste a business can make is of time. The businesses do it so often that they don't even regard it as a waste. They take it for granted.

Every material waste can be salvaged but no amount of time can ever be salvaged once it is gone it can never come back. The truth is Lean Six Sigma can help a business put the time to efficient use, so understanding the methodology is a smart choice for any business. The outcomes will be rewarding for any business making a business reach its maximum output with minimum wastage.

Our Business is not that big

The most common voice raise against Six Sigma by Mid and Small-sized businesses is that they consider that their organization is not a large corporation to implement Six Sigma. The solution here is that Six Sigma won't be applied in a day and show the results immediately. Following its principles will show benefits sooner and an improve infrastructure will come forward. Six Sigma will make it easier to understand customers' needs and work according to it.

Once the key wastages are identified in any business it becomes easy to use them in the DMAIC framework. Time management gets easier to handle tasks that were taking longer periods of time. It is to understand that Six Sigma methodologies are there to improve the overall processing of the company by utilizing every material and reducing waste. The size of the organization doesn't matter at all as it benefits all.

We aren't manufacturing anything

While the Six Sigma methodology was born in the manufacturing industry it has left a greater impact on services and transactions environment also. Many people think that its parent organization is a manufacturing company thus it can produce the results only in the manufacturing environment. This is a total misconception as the Lean Six Sigma methodologies can equally be used in the companies that offer services only.

The services industries need it more than anything as their product is intangible and the work done is in a repetitive process in a large volume. Delivering, invoicing, order processing, employee onboarding, accounts payable, all of this can become smooth to handle with the help of Six Sigma methodology.

We used Six Sigma in the past but the results weren't good enough

Defining success here is really important and finding the reasons for Six Sigma failure are more important.

- Were the processes tracked and shared properly?

- Was the communication between managers up to date?

- Were the employees were trained to use the tools?

- Were the leaders committed to the program?

- Was the program internally driven?

- Was it in the context of people or technology?

- Were the employees aware that you were launching such a program?

- Were the goals realistically set?

- How the projects were chosen?

- Were the projects managed carefully?

Before raising the question against Six Sigma, evaluating the reasons for adopting Six Sigma are more important. Six Sigma methodology will work efficiently according to the efforts of the people implementing it. It is a commitment amongst all the levels of a corporation including front line supervisors. Six Sigma is a culture that is adopted gradually by the whole organization. It is not something that should be the duty of one sector only. Failure to accept the change could be one reason of malfunctioning.

We find Lean more appropriate for our business than Six Sigma

Six Sigma and Lean production complement each other running side by side along with other concepts. Where lean simplifies business by eliminating waste and getting more from less, Six Sigma refines the process making it near perfect. The Lean can be stated as an efficient method, the Six Sigma can be stated as an effective method. Combining effectiveness and efficiency a company can get great results. With the use of Lean production only you are sacrificing the perfect quality while adopting Six Sigma only you reduce the chance of efficiency. Hence, both concepts run side to side complementing one another.

Conclusion

Throughout history, there has always been a need for improvement in every aspect of life. There had been alterations and maturity that had opened new dimensions of success. Improvement is evident in everything that a man has achieved so far.

Organizations are also learning; in every era, there is something new to work on. From the beginning, the individuals and organizations are seeking improved operating methods that not only save time but also the efforts, resources, and cost.

The culture of organizations has been changed completely over time because of the successful constant improvement methods that are developed to benefit the organization and its employees. This new culture is vital in putting a desire in the mind of the members of the organization to focus on the strategies that improve the operations of the unit and yields better results.

Lean Six Sigma is developed from two separate but very much alike improvement methods: Lean and Six Sigma. Although there is a lot of difference in how both methodologies help to attain the organization's goal, both have the same aim i.e. to improve the processing. Both methods when combined produce a better outcome than the one method alone.

Although recognized by some big names in the market, combining Lean and Six Sigma together is not easy and how will it proceed to depend upon your organization. How the Lean Six Sigma should be implemented in any organization depends on its culture and leadership. The initial experiences might not produce the perfect results as practice makes perfect with time.

The effectiveness of the combination of both methods is evident from the experience of the companies who have gained the benefits from them. Though there is a lot of research already conducted on the matter, still more research will be able to identify the problems and challenges that an organization might face. Research should be conducted for every sector separately to give an insight of Six Sigma implementation.

As we are over with our journey with you to guide you with 'Lean Six Sigma Methodologies' we have high hopes for you that may it be a great beginning for you. The book has defined all the basics you needed to get started with Lean Six Sigma in your organization. Some of the points have been so repeatedly defined with various angles that the reader finally gets a feeling that I already know that. The journey you are about to take is a long one with something new to learn on every step but before we close this book for good let us look into the aspects that will give a brief overview of the book.

Through time the human mind has achieved so much just because of a single idea. The idea which is generally born out of a need, as we say that "need is the mother of invention", has a snowball effect that rolls down a hill building and gathering up other ideas along with it and eventually getting bigger and bigger with no stop. The same can be said for Six Sigma which started as a methodology to implement and reduce the defects to 3.4 per million opportunities is running alongside other concepts. Along the way, Six Sigma was combined with lean production to result in Lean Six Sigma making it a perfect process with least wastage.

The lean production method contributed to reducing wastage of different types. Where Lean Six Sigma is considered to be a methodology for manufacturing processes, it can also be used in the services industry. Most of the time businesses fail to recognize that they actually need Six Sigma which leads to one problem after another. Six Sigma is the answer to problems most of the time as it helps to understand the root cause of the problem and finding an effective solution for it.

Six Sigma focuses on a much greater aspect which is the customer. A happy customer is a happy business. Every customer has his own needs and satisfaction, realizing the needs of a customer is what a Six Sigma certification can help with. Once certified, an individual gains the knowledge of understanding the customer and making it clear to the production line.

Failure and mistakes are what make a man perfect but for the company, the same couldn't be said much. As a company failure means to put one's reputation at stake, no one likes to do so. Sadly, few businesses seem to work their way towards failure without realizing, the reason is the failure to understand what a customer needs.

Lean Six Sigma has also been criticized by businesses but it has been so because businesses failed to recognize what Lean Six Sigma actually is. Hiring a Master Black Belt Six Sigma professional for training the company employees is a smart way to see what it can do for you.

Most of the time, businesses forget that Lean Six Sigma is a step by step process which requires working or focus on a single project than getting into all the things at once. Working in a descending order to solve the problems with Lean Six Sigma methodology is recommended as it fills up the gaps that cause production delays in the first place. Implementing Six Sigma isn't a one day job; instead, it requires assurance, attention, seriousness, and dedication to get the job done.

The Japanese manufacturers are praised worldwide when it comes to quality management as the processes like Kaizen and Genchi Genbutsu brought reforms of their own. The concept of day to day continuous improvement contributed towards handling small problems one at a time and leading to corrections in the overall process.

The concept of paying respect to employees and understanding them as a key factor of production brought revolution in thinking of managers all over the world. The employees were now working with higher morale and contributing more towards quality on the whole.

By having a new perspective towards the company's structure and understanding the role of front line supervisors, manufacturers were able to have noticeable gains in terms of profit. Investing in training of employees resulted in lower turnover increasing the overall stability of the employees.

Listening to employees and giving them the training they wanted to change the outlook of employees towards companies giving them a sense of security.

Once employees get to know that they are the number one priority for the company, everyone started working with extra dedication resulting in a decrease in the overall production process. And this is what Lean Six Sigma aims to achieve.

References

Chapter I: The Origin of Six Sigma

- (Griffin, A Short History of the British Industrial Revolution, 2010)
- Webber, Larry; Wallace, Michael (15 December 2006). Quality Control for Dummies. For Dummies. pp. 42–43. Retrieved 2019-10-30.
- Snee, R. D. (2004). Six-Sigma: the evolution of 100 years of business. *International Journal of Six Sigma and Competitive Advantage, 1*(1), 4-20.
- Soderborg, N. R. (2004, November). Design for six sigma at Ford. In Six Sigma Forum Magazine (Vol. 4, No. 1). ASQ.
- Boudreaux, D. J., & Holcombe, R. G. (1989). The Coasian and Knightian theories of the firm. *Managerial and Decision Economics (1986-1998), 10*(2), 61.
- Eckes, G. (2002). *The Six Sigma revolution: How General Electric and others turned process into profits*. John Wiley & Sons.
- Johnson, N. L., Kotz, S., & Wu, X. Z. (1991). Inspection errors for attributes in quality control (Vol. 44). CRC Press.
- Paul Brunet, A., & New, S. (2003). Kaizen in Japan: an empirical study. *International Journal of Operations & Production Management, 23*(12), 1426-1446.

- *Imai, Masaaki, 1930-. (1986). Kaizen (Ky'zen), the key to Japan's competitive success. New York :Random House Business Division,*

- Arnheiter, E. D., & Maleyeff, J. (2005). The integration of lean management and Six Sigma. The TQM magazine, 17(1), 5-18.

- Ohno, T. (1988). Toyota production system: beyond large-scale production. crc Press.

- Dahlgaard, J. J., & Mi Dahlgaard-Park, S. (2006). Lean production, six sigma quality, TQM and company culture. The TQM magazine, 18(3), 263-281.

- Rafaeli, A. (1985). Quality circles and employee attitudes. Personnel Psychology, 38(3), 603-615.

- Ohno, T. (1982). How the Toyota production system was created. Japanese Economic Studies, 10(4), 83-101.

- Krafcik, J. F. (1988). Triumph of the lean production system. MIT Sloan Management Review, 30(1), 41.

- Eckes, G. (2002). The Six Sigma revolution: How General Electric and others turned process into profits. John Wiley & Sons.

- Caulcutt, R. (2001). Why is Six Sigma so successful?. Journal of Applied Statistics, 28(3-4), 301-306.

- Harry, M. J. (1998). Six Sigma: a breakthrough strategy for profitability. Quality progress, 31(5), 60.

Chapter II: Being Open to Change as a Business

- Clegg, B., Wang, T., & Ji, P. (2010). Understanding customer needs through quantitative analysis of Kano's model. *International Journal of Quality & Reliability Management*.
- Shahin, A. (2004). Integration of FMEA and the Kano model: An exploratory examination. *International Journal of Quality & Reliability Management, 21(7)*, 731-746.
- Mikulić, J., & Prebežac, D. (2011). A critical review of techniques for classifying quality attributes in the Kano model. *Managing*

Service Quality: An International Journal, *21*(1), 46-66.

- Bayus, B. L. (2008). Understanding customer needs. *Handbook of Technology and Innovation Management*, 115-142.
- Gee, R., Coates, G., & Nicholson, M. (2008). Understanding and profitably managing customer loyalty. *Marketing Intelligence & Planning*, *26*(4), 359-374.
- Du, X., Jiao, J., & Tseng, M. M. (2003). Identifying customer need patterns for customization and personalization. *Integrated manufacturing systems*, *14*(5), 387-396.
- Meyer, C., & Schwager, A. (2007). Understanding customer experience. *Harvard business review*, *85*(2), 116.
- Pugh, A. J. (2009). *Longing and belonging: Parents, children, and consumer culture*. Univ of California Press.
- Ward, S., Wackman, D. B., & Wartella, E. (1977). *How children learn to buy: The development of consumer information-processing skills*. Sage.
- Dahlgaard, J. J., & Mi Dahlgaard-Park, S. (2006). Lean production, six sigma quality, TQM and company culture. The TQM magazine, 18(3), 263-281.
- Anderson, E. W. (1998). Customer satisfaction and word of mouth. *Journal of service research*, *1*(1), 5-17.

- George, M. (2002). *Lean Six Sigma, Chapter 2 - Six Sigma: The Power of Culture.* McGraw Hill Professional.

- Gupta, D. (2015). *Success Using Lean Six Sigma in Terms of Operations and Business Processes.* Anchor Academic Publishing.

- Tennant, G. (2017). *Six Sigma: SPC and TQM in Manufacturing and Services.* Taylor & Francis.

- Terence T. Burton, J. L. (2005). *Six Sigma for Small and Mid-sized Organizations: Success Through Scaleable Deployment.* J. Ross Publishing.

Chapter III: Looking from Customer's Perspective

- File, K. M., & Prince, R. A. (1992). Positive word-of-mouth: customer satisfaction and buyer behaviour. *International Journal of Bank Marketing, 10*(1), 25-29.
- Hines, P., Rich, N., Bicheno, J., Brunt, D., Taylor, D., Butterworth, C., & Sullivan, J. (1998). Value stream management. *The International Journal of Logistics Management, 9*(1), 25-42.
- Chen, J. C., Li, Y., & Shady, B. D. (2010). From value stream mapping toward a lean/sigma continuous improvement process: an industrial case study. *International Journal of Production Research, 48*(4), 1069-1086.
- Teichgräber, U. K., & de Bucourt, M. (2012). Applying value stream mapping techniques to eliminate non-value-added waste for the procurement of endovascular stents. *European journal of radiology, 81*(1), e47-e52.
- Pepper, M. P., & Spedding, T. A. (2010). The evolution of lean Six Sigma. *International Journal*

of *Quality & Reliability Management*, *27*(2), 138-155.

- Haefner, B., Kraemer, A., Stauss, T., & Lanza, G. (2014). Quality value stream mapping. *Procedia Cirp*, *17*, 254-259.
- Snee, R. D. (2005). When worlds collide: lean and six sigma. *Quality Progress*, *38*(9), 63-65.
- Hines, Peter & Rich, Nick. (1997). The seven value stream mapping tools. International Journal of Operations & Production Management. 17. 46-64. 10.1108/01443579710157989.
- McKechnie, S. (1992). Consumer buying behaviour in financial services: an overview. *International Journal of Bank Marketing*, *10*(5), 5-39.
- Hill, R. W., & Hillier, T. J. (1977). *Organizational buying behaviour*. Springer.
- Jaakkola, E. (2007). Purchase decision-making within professional consumer services: organizational or consumer buying behaviour. *Marketing Theory*, *7*(1), 93-108.
- Valentine, V., & Gordon, W. (2000). The 21st century consumer: a new model of thinking. *International Journal of Market Research*, *42*(2), 1-16.
- Bils, M., & Klenow, P. J. (1998). Using consumer theory to test competing business cycles models. *Journal of Political Economy*, *106*(2), 233-261.

Chapter IV: The Core Methodologies of Six Sigma

- Pepper, M. P., & Spedding, T. A. (2010). The evolution of lean Six Sigma. *International Journal of Quality & Reliability Management, 27*(2), 138-155.

- Dahlgaard, J. J., & Mi Dahlgaard-Park, S. (2006). Lean production, six sigma quality, TQM and company culture. *The TQM magazine, 18*(3), 263-281.

- Kumar, D. (2006). Six Sigma Best Practices: A Guide to Business Process Excellence for Diverse Industries. J. Ross Publishing.
- Rasmusson, D. (2006). SIPOC Picture Book: A Visual Guide to SIPOC/DMAIC Relationship. Oriel Incorporated.
- Shankar, R. (2009). Process Improvement Using Six Sigma: A DMAIC Guide. ASQ Quality Press.
- Thomas McCarty, L. D. (2004). The Six Sigma Black Belt Handbook, Chapter 18 - DMADV, Part 18. McGraw Hill Professional.
- Seow, C., & Antony, J. (2004). Some pros and cons of Six Sigma: an academic perspective. *The TQM magazine.*
- Cronemyr, P. (2007). DMAIC and DMADV-differences, similarities and synergies. *International Journal of Six Sigma and Competitive Advantage, 3*(3), 193-209.
- Selvi, K., & Majumdar, R. (2014). Six sigma-overview of DMAIC and DMADV. *International Journal of Innovative Science and Modern Engineering, 2*(5), 16-19.
- Tonini, A. C., Spinola, M. D. M., & Laurindo, F. J. B. (2006, July). Six Sigma and software development process: DMAIC improvements. In *2006 Technology Management for the Global Future-PICMET 2006 Conference* (Vol. 6, pp. 2815-2823). IEEE.

- Mandal, P. (2012). Improving process improvement: executing the analyze and improve phases of DMAIC better. *International Journal of Lean Six Sigma*, *3*(3), 231-250.
- Soković, M., Jovanović, J., Krivokapić, Z., & Vujović, A. (2009). Basic quality tools in continuous improvement process. *Journal of Mechanical Engineering*, *55*(5), 1-9.

- Karen Martin, M. O. (2013). *Value Stream Mapping: How to Visualize Work and Align Leadership for Organizational Transformation: How to Visualize Work and Align Leadership for Organizational Transformation.* McGraw Hill Professional.

- Locher, D. A. (2008). *Value Stream Mapping for Lean Development: A How-To Guide for Streamlining Time to Market.* CRC Press.

- Mark A. Nash, S. R. (2011). *Mapping the Total Value Stream: A Comprehensive Guide for Production and Transactional Processes.* CRC Press.

- Mike Rother, J. S. (2003). *Learning to See: Value Stream Mapping to Add Value and Eliminate Muda.* Lean Enterprise Institute.

Chapter V: Adopting and Modifying Six Sigma for Use

- Shimbun, N. K. (1989). Poka-yoke: Improving product quality by preventing defects. Productivity Press.
- Van Iwaarden, J., van der Wiele, T., Dale, B., Williams, R., & Bertsch, B. (2008). The Six Sigma improvement approach: a transnational comparison. International Journal of Production Research, 46(23), 6739-6758.
- Linderman, K., Schroeder, R. G., & Choo, A. S. (2006). Six Sigma: the role of goals in improvement teams. Journal of operations Management, 24(6), 779-790.
- Thawani, S. (2004). Six sigma—strategy for organizational excellence. Total Quality Management & Business Excellence, 15(5-6), 655-664.

- Michael George, J. M. (2004). The Lean Six Sigma Pocket Toolbook. McGraw Hill Professional.
- Sarkar, D. (2004). Lessons in Six Sigma: 72 Must-Know Truths for Managers. SAGE Publications India.
- Antony, J. (2002). Design for Six Sigma: a breakthrough business improvement strategy for achieving competitive advantage. Work Study, 51(1), 6-8.
- Vinod, M., Devadasan, S. R., Sunil, D. T., & Thilak, V. M. M. (2015). Six Sigma through Poka-Yoke: a navigation through literature arena. The International Journal of Advanced Manufacturing Technology, 81(1-4), 315-327.
- Dudek-Burlikowska, M., & Szewieczek, D. (2009). The Poka-Yoke method as an improving quality tool of operations in the process. Journal of Achievements in Materials and Manufacturing Engineering, 36(1), 95-102.

- Cary Adams, P. G. (2007). *Six Sigma Deployment.* Routledge.

- Shimbun, N. K. (1989). *Poka-Yoke: Improving Product Quality by Preventing Defects.* CRC Press.

Shingo, S. (1986). *Zero Quality Control: Source Inspection and the Poka-Yoke System.* CRC Press

-

Chapter VI: Six Sigma Certification and Criticism

- Burton, T. T. (2011). *Accelerating Lean Six Sigma Results: How to Achieve Improvement Excellence in the New Economy.* J. Ross Publishing.

- T. M. Kubiak, D. W. (2009). *The Certified Six Sigma Black Belt Handbook.* ASQ Quality Press.

- Antony, J., Jiju Antony, F., Kumar, M., & Rae Cho, B. (2007). Six sigma in service organisations: Benefits, challenges and difficulties, common myths, empirical observations and success factors. *International journal of quality & reliability management, 24*(3), 294-311.
- Dahlgaard-Park, S. M., & Bendell, T. (2006). A review and comparison of six sigma and the lean organisations. *The TQM magazine.*
- Kumar, M., Antony, J., Antony, F. J., & Madu, C. N. (2007). Winning customer loyalty in an automotive company through Six Sigma: a case study. *Quality and Reliability Engineering International, 23*(7), 849-866.

- Antony, J. (2006). Six sigma for service processes. *Business process management journal, 12*(2), 234-248.

- Baird, C. (2009). *The Six Sigma Manual for Small and Medium Businesses: What You Need to Know Explained Simply.* Atlantic Publishing Company.

- George, M. L. (2003). *Lean Six Sigma for Service: How to Use Lean Speed and Six Sigma Quality to Improve Services and Transactions.* McGraw Hill Professional.

- Muralidharan, K. (2015). *Six Sigma for Organizational Excellence: A Statistical Approach.* Springer.

- Tennant, G. (2017). *Six Sigma: SPC and TQM in Manufacturing and Services.* Taylor & Francis.

- Tina Agustiady, A. B. (2012). *Sustainability: Utilizing Lean Six Sigma Techniques.* CRC Press.

Truscott, W. (2012). *Six Sigma.* Routledge

-